The

Moral Now

The

Moral Now

A Martial Art of Parenting

Brett Jordan

ENP · A Canadian Publisher

First printing, 2018. Printed in the United States.

Visit www.brettjordanspace.com

ISBN: 978-1-7752888-1-7

17 7 5 2 8 8 8 1 7

Elevate Now Publishing

To my longsuffering family,

Yiskah, Asher, Jacob and Noah.

From the bottom of my heart,

thank you.

Contents

1

Right Now

"Like arrows in the hand of a warrior, so are the children of one's youth. Happy is the man who has his quiver full of them; they shall not be ashamed, but shall speak with their enemies in the gate."

- Psalm 127:4-5

There's a wide gulf between the basic act of parenting and actually *being* a parent. In my mind, the term "parenting" can easily apply to any standard of care, regardless of whether it's actually functional or not. The term is nothing more than a loaded verb; an action which can be just as carelessly and mindlessly carried out in the same manner as sweeping dust off the floor, wringing out a wet towel, or pumping gas. Parenting itself, therefore, does not necessarily imply positive or negative actions. It is simply one of those vacuum words, the content of which is left decidedly open-ended.

Mindfully *being* the parent, however, is a completely different thing. It implies taking a distinctive ownership of the action which ultimately leads to an organic, meaningful transformation - principally for the parent him or herself. It is the essential immersion into, and the embracing of, the tangible *now* of a parent's experience and the ability to recognize the present moment as distinct from the larger, and often more distracting, story of life.

Being the parent means allowing the integrity of *right now* - that precious, singular moment of awareness - to inform a person of much higher things, and for that moment to guide them through the unpredictable chaos of disorder and constant change that is a natural part of family life.

In many ways, family dynamics are a free-flowing phenomenon of individualized passions, diverse opinions and frequently-diverging perspectives that are all culminating within the intimate space of a single household. Somehow, the parent is called upon to manage these things in a healthy and functional way that facilitates some sense of order while also preserving the unique temperaments and tenors of each child. Many parents succeed in this task, while many others stumble hopelessly, never quite able to gain their footing.

While it has been often stated that the family unit is the basic building block of society, I recognize that this assertion has received some criticism over the recent past. This is because we live in a time where the definition of "family" is being forced into new filters of progressive lenses and, as such, the value that was once attributed to the roles of both mother and father has taken some pretty hard hits. While being no assassin to the ideals of human progress, I remain nevertheless convinced that there is an inimitable aspect of family life that serves to train both child and parent in the much larger facets of global cooperation.

In other words, there is a dance taking place in this very sacred little community that we call family; a dance which, in all its wonderful blend of movement, motion and vibration, is designed to instill the most conscious form of responsibility in those who are a part of it.

This is one of the reasons why I see parenting – in its most pristine expressions – as a type of martial art form which can have a profound impact on the very culture of our world.

Yet the onus is on us, the parents, to carry this forward.

The martial arts are associated with a concept of war; of military strategies and elite defense techniques that stand the test of time in terms of their powerful application. While it may sound a little strange to refer to parenting as a martial art (unless your mind goes to the all-too familiar experience of battling with your own children), I would firmly argue that the war we are really talking about here is one of overcoming a more insidious type of adversary that we are all facing in terms of our collective species. It is the transcendence of something far more complex than the physical threat of the proverbial *other*.

It is the battle against your own self.

The war we are referring to here is the one we are daily waging in the context of our conditioned, personal selves. This is the war against mediocrity, against tepid standards and a lazy adherence to what we would publically proclaim to be our values – yet quietly ignore for the sake of behavioral convenience. Essentially, this is the battle to overcome the deflated state of our baseline human behavior, and to ultimately allow for the victorious emerging of our fuller, more awakened self.

It is not by mere coincidence that the Hebrew Bible tells us that we were made in the "image and likeness" of the Creator. As human history has shown to us through countless recycled anecdotes, however, our experience of that "likeness" has not been altogether visible or easily attained, for that matter. Rather, the classical experience of the human life has been marked by such recurring and universal themes such as panic, frustration, greed, desperation, anger and complete disorientation (those being some of the more digestible ones). Yet, every now and then we are morally, albeit briefly, awakened from our sedated baseline through the pioneering example of people who have occasionally broken the mass-produced standard of human behavior, and who have demonstrated something far better than what our daily experience would actually tell us we're capable of. Every once in a while our attention is struck by the valor of a man or a woman who was somehow able to defy the cultural, social and political expectations thrust upon each of us, and who actually began to walk in the opposite direction of everybody else. Those are the types of people that we remember.

The truest figures who have behaved this way are the real pioneers among us; the ones who have sincerely approached mastery in their occupation of humanity. These are the ones who, rather than being so preoccupied with controlling others or deceitfully manipulating the material realities of their particular circumstances, instead decided to develop and alter their own human responses as well as allow their most cherished beliefs to mature in the face of those challenging situations. These are the people who are the greatest martial artists, for the very reason that they continue to practice a mastery over that most insidious of opponents, the *sleeping* self. As Giordano Bruno put it, *"the Divine Light is always in man, presenting itself to the senses and to the comprehension, but man rejects it."*

Experiences such as these compel us to turn our minds back to the primordial design of our species, and to consider that we have been breathed into existence for the very object of leading our earth with the tools of a fuller, more eternal Divine Consciousness. Behavior and conduct that exemplifies this higher consciousness is what our human baseline is actually supposed to look like.

With that said, I should point out that this is not a book about parenting *strategies*. I don't consider myself nearly well-adjusted enough in my own parenting to presume to be able to teach others how to do it, particularly since – at the time of this writing – my own children are still very young and I have yet to witness the actual fruit of their independence. For parenting expertise, there are plenty of books already out there, written by people who probably know far more about what they're doing than I do, and who are more than happy to bring out the latest pop research on how to make your child listen, behave, sleep and use the toilet properly.

So rather than being a book about raising *kids*, this book is more about raising one's own consciousness and awareness, specifically within the very context of being a parent and all of the uncertainty that comes along with it. As such, this is a book for the humbled parent – the type who has enough sense of self-effacement to be able to accept new learning and quiet wisdom. It's especially written for the parent who has enough honesty to recognize their own moments of being like that proverbial deer caught in the headlights, and who are able to admit that they don't know what they are doing.

How refreshing it can be to just *say* that.

One of the recurring themes you will find in these pages is the importance of feeling centered and grounded while engaged in the everyday fluctuations of family life. This means claiming and owning your space as a mother or father, and taking the steps needed to make that space as healthy and flexible as possible while holding true to your personal standards and values. Ultimately, the goal here is that your natural love for your child *and* your independently-chosen parenting approaches are able to meet each other peacefully, without all of the glaring fault lines that are prominent in so many dysfunctional homes today.

It will be emphasized more than once, however, that the principle of being centered and awakened as a practitioner of the martial art does not preclude the likelihood of routine chaos and stress in the home. Rather, the practice of centering will be elaborated and revisited throughout these pages specifically *because* such things are a reality for most of us. Just as we cannot control the worldview of others, it is equally true that we cannot guarantee the specific paths and interpretations that our children will make in their particular life. While I would still argue that we can play a fundamental role in guiding and helping to inform the perspectives of others – be it our children or anybody else - I would caution that this is most effectively done when we are able to self-monitor and self-reflect on a regular basis. As the object of this book underscores, the most potent change in the world is the one which transpires deep within the heart of him who knows that change is necessary in the first place. If I can put it another way, I would say that our responsibility is to change ourselves first, before we begin putting that kind of expectation on anyone else. And once we've made that necessary change…then we need to change it again. And again.

Many consciousness-seeking parents have questioned whether it's even possible to be in the "now" when simultaneously being the subject of endless demands and needs from a growing child. As any parent can attest, the true reality is that quite often children simply don't leave you alone. Being in the *now* of human consciousness, while it can easily be regarded as a distant luxury for the contemporary parent, is nevertheless one of the most important things that today's parent can do – both for themselves as well as for their child. In this way, the perspective I'm sharing in this book may be seen as a paradoxical one, particularly in the sense that conscious awakening is not an *exception* to the realities of raising children, but rather should be a natural, necessary product of it.

If I can take it a step further, parenting provides one of the most colorful and vibrant contexts for personal transformation, if we simply allow it to be so.   After all, our highest calling is to bring service to others and to ultimately foster growth and healing in the earth. What better training ground for such excellent standards of co-leadership, then, than the raw and rugged terrain of raising a child? This is the territory that will forge a true moral artist, so long as one is willing to follow this path in all of its glorious twists and turns; ultimately allowing the rawness of the journey to shape and refine the diligent seeker.

To that extent, there is nothing in these pages that I have not personally taken to heart for myself, as well as applied in my own life. With that said, if there is anything that I will ultimately be able to give my own children by way of actual, authentic service as a parent over the course of my phase as a father, I believe it will simply be to have enough self-transparency to accept the fact that I may not have been what they always needed while they were growing up – particularly in their earliest developmental years while I was still floundering hopelessly - and to simply accept this as a sobering reality while continuing to pursue healing change in myself.

At the very least, my capacity to accept that I had not learned what I wanted to learn early enough in life may be, in itself, a new beginning that I can build on and hopefully serve as a catalyst in forming new bonds with my children. 'Better late than never,' as they say. Yet even as I write that sentence I can actually recognize the fatalistic implications of it, especially because it implies that something valuable was lost and that any hope for moving forward involves having to 'salvage' something else from the wreckage. With this in mind, perhaps the better and healthier way to frame the clumsiness of my early parenting years is to recognize the fact that my child was brought into my life as the most fundamental and beautiful form of training for a greater way of being. Furthermore, it can be said that every one of my children was entirely necessary for my own redirection from faulty beliefs and egoic expectations about life. Indeed, my children were my own schoolmasters for learning about paths of higher living, which is why – for all of us – they are really not intended to come into our lives once we are comfortably 'established' but rather as a way of being an establishing essence in our lives. They lead us back to where we need to go. So long as we're willing to be led, that is.

For my part, I awake each day with the resolve to remain open to what I need to learn in order to be the best version of myself for this task. The journey has to be *now*.

The embracing of now will have a singular influence on where I will be *later*.

In that sense, I suppose you could say that this is a book that reflects more on *bad* parenting, rather than on good parenting. If anything, I'm certainly more experienced in the former arena than I am with the latter. I'm just thankful for the wake-up call that took place while my kids were still quite young, before the effects of my own unconscious pathology were able to go on without being thoughtfully addressed. Meditation practice has been a vital part of this realization, and once I started doing this I was instantly shocked over the fact that I had not considered taking up the practice a long time ago.

Suffice it to say that I know enough about meditation in order to get through my own day, and whatever little knowledge I have in this area has simply been born out of a few short years of being a busy parent while attempting to navigate the monolithic contours of the "meaning of life," so to speak. If I were to strive to write a whole book about meditation, its conclusion would probably be right about here, a few pages into the manuscript. With that said, if you want quality instruction or deeper insight about meditation, I would say you are more likely to find it by simply taking an hour to sit alone with yourself than by searching through these pages.

A word about spirituality as well, if you will permit me.

I have come to find that the term 'spirituality' covers an area that is about as broad as east is from west, and for that reason can be applied to the personal philosophy of the homeless opiate addict just as easily to the Jesuit Priest or the Tibetan monk. While my own personal views are biblically-based, I'm conscious enough to understand that theistic perspectives do not hold a monopoly on the term "spiritual" in today's world. In my opinion, there are virtually countless words in our collective body of spiritual commentary that all serve to inform those who are seeking enlightenment, yet at the end of the day every person's spirituality is theirs to discover and theirs to build a personal relationship with. As Gandhi himself put it so succinctly, *"God has no religion."*

I will point out, however, that most major religions or spiritual cultures that have spanned our human history have been underscored by one very common and universal theme. Very simply, it has been the virtue of *love*. Love that ultimately transcends every fault, every injustice, and everything else that we struggle with in our quest to undertake this thing called "life." Unconditional, self-absolving love is what yields Divine reconciliation both in a divided self as well as in a divided world, and its very practice is the thing that tends towards ultimate atonement in the universal realm of things. It fosters an alignment of the highest order which, when practiced in consistent measure, leads to a very sweet and satisfying human experience that is nothing short of a spiritual experience.

If this book is about anything in particular, I suppose you could say that it's a personal reflection on the nature of *awakening*, written from the perspective of a husband and father with a little too much experience with failure, yet also much to give in terms of sincere advice on the importance of embracing the values of stillness and thoughtful space in the progressive and pioneer-like trail of guiding children through this world.

Every parent is a student of the vocation itself, and some become masters of the art while others remain stagnant in their experience of it; unable to fully orient themselves within the sheer messiness and unpredictability of that world. The latter ones seem to find it hard to practice the craft without facilitating some kind of lasting injury to themselves – often identifying the culprit of the pain as parenting itself – while the former have somehow figured out (often without even realizing it) that the process of bringing a child into the world both biologically and emotionally is actually one of life's greatest manifestations for personal discovery and growth as a human being. It is the realization that the concept of 'surviving it' needs to be transcended by the simple art of immersing yourself in it; and being ultimately transformed by what it is offering you. It is to know that there is nothing that needs escaping from in the world of parenting, other than your pre-conceived expectations.

In other words, the successful ones - if any parent can be deemed that - are those who received the experience in such a way where they remained open to the transformative effect it would have on their ego. These are the ones who allow themselves the graceful freedom to be wonderfully fermented by its complex and inexplicable processes, and to thereby become greater human beings as a result. To use the words of Leonardo Da Vinci, *"one can have no smaller or greater mastery than mastery of oneself."*

In conclusion, the words in these pages are written for those who are seeking a higher plane of existence than the mere status quo of 'Parenting 101.' It is intended for mothers and fathers (and also those who are on the path toward these beautiful vocations) who have a burning desire to never stop transforming, and to ultimately be the best version of themselves that they possibly can.

It is my fond hope that this book may be of service to such people.

Peace and blessings.

2

The Pathology of Story

5am.

Dedicated, I pull myself out of bed with the anticipation
of sitting at my laptop, researching and writing, striving
to immerse myself into the sweet flow of information
that I regretfully shunned throughout the majority of my
youth. As far as my twenties were concerned, that was a
time for fun, for socializing in various nondescript and
pointless forms, for eating garbage, watching garbage,
thinking garbage, and for generally just being at ease in
my overall ignorance of the world.

Fast-forward, then, to my marriage, my early years as a
husband, and ultimately my unstable, confusing and
hopelessly clumsy start as a father where I basically
stumbled over myself right out of the gate. To this day, I
sometimes feel as though I've barely just picked myself
up off the ground, and have merely caught glimpses of
my potential as the husband and father I aspire to be.

Despite our many years together, my wife Yiskah and I only began to carve out a purposeful pattern for our mornings after our oldest child was about six years old. I have ultimately developed a morning routine which I've been excited to sink my teeth into, and was gifted to be able to fully launch into it once I was laid off from my job. A few years back I had the blessing of several months to become familiar with my morning sanctuary of space; tweaking it, adjusting it, and trimming it down to a reasonable, family-friendly proportion until I eventually had to return to my work and was then able to incorporate it into my regular weekly schedule with only a moderate amount of congestion.

We basically set ourselves to this task in order to take some thoughtful ownership over our little corner of the world. After all, it seems that for so long the culture we live in has been getting hungrier and hungrier for our better parts, and has appeared to satiate itself on devouring up all remnants of integrity within our marriage and in our relationship with our children. For this reason, I knew I needed to address the effect that this was having on my family. So with that in mind, in our household I simply started by getting up *early*.

Without a doubt, I never regret getting up earlier than my children, no matter how tired I might be. There is something so utterly majestic and empowering about the morning hour that defies words. To me, it is truly a transformative hour in the way that it fosters a sense of realignment with higher purpose while simultaneously creating a serene space for quiet contemplation. There is nothing like a crisp, dark morning to feed the soul's deepest needs in advance of the day's perpetual barrage of demands and deadlines – the very same things that often make us forget we even *have* a soul.

Mornings are sacred.

Henry David Thoreau, in his book *Walden*, beautifully captured the magnificent love affair that one is capable of having with this universal and natural phenomenon called morning. And he would know too, for he spent two years of his life living in quiet solitude in a single-room cabin in the woods, purposely applying himself to meditative reflection. For him, the experience of being fully immersed in the earliest morning hour was akin to nothing less than a feeling of camaraderie with the heavenly host, and a journey into the deepest reaches of the cosmos.

"I got up early and bathed in the pond; that was a religious exercise, and one of the best things which I did. They say that characters were engraven on the bathing tub of King Tching-thang to this effect: 'Renew thyself completely each day; do it again, and again, and forever again.' I can understand that. Morning brings back the heroic ages....There was something cosmical about it; a standing advertisement, till forbidden, of the everlasting vigor and fertility of the world. The morning, which is the most memorable season of the day, is the awakening hour. Then there is least somnolence in us; and for an hour, at least, some part of us awakes which slumbers all the rest of the day and night."

My mornings are fairly simple and straightforward, for that matter, which is how I like it. I won't go into too much detail as to my personal regiment here – since it is likely to change over time – though I will share that I basically stagger my mornings with a dedicated, physical workout one day with a quiet journaling session the next. I meditate and pray, and I incorporate a period of gratefulness. On my smoother days, I manage to complete this cycle without a single stirring from my kids. Yet many days aren't like this…

For now, however, this is how I greet the rising of the sun in our household. This is my modus operandi for laying claim to the life that I want for myself and our children. This is how I am working at preparing my mind, first thing in the morning, so that I feel equipped to take ownership of the rest of the day, rather than having the day own me. And it's all well and good, of course, until a monkey wrench is thrown into the works.

To that effect, here's how today's morning unfolds.

5:15 am. Our eldest, Asher, is already awake, and I can hear him in the hallway, insisting to my wife that he isn't tired (the little Aries that he is). The deal is that he is allowed to be out of bed only if he stays in his room, engaged in a quiet activity, so that mom and dad can have some focus time for the first hour of the day. At 6 am, however, all bets are off, and it's about as much as he can manage to stay in there for that long.

He promptly joins me at the table where I'm busy working on my current project. There are times where he occupies himself with some other activity, but today he pulls his chair right next to mine and fixes his eyes on the intoxicating glow of the laptop. I'm not a big fan of endorsing too much screen time for our kids (we don't even have a TV in our house), but these morning hours have become very precious to me, particularly since our boys don't typically fall asleep in the evening until well after our best energies are exhausted. And given the fact that we get up as early as we do, working late into the night is not really an option at this stage.

Thankfully, what I'm occupied in is something my son can benefit from. An audio translation from English into Hebrew of the book of Genesis.

While his intense little presence jars me from my meditative zone of study, it goes without saying that his inquisitions into what I'm writing are serving to teach him something valuable and spiritually-informative. Shifting endlessly in his chair, bumping my hands as they're typing, and constantly asking me to go back to the previous screens so he can softly mouth the Hebrew sounds from the reference page, *he* is now the one who has entered a zone, and I'm the one helping to facilitate it for him.

Ultimately, the time is well spent – even though my intention was to reserve the whole hour exclusively for myself. For now, however, this is good. I'm showing him something that I believe will serve him well in his growth and learning, and we're starting our day together, just him and I. Best of all, being laid off from my day job permits me the rare luxury of being able to do this without the added panic of rushing out the door.

The rest of our morning, however, is generally spent putting out our children's fires as we struggle to move meaningfully through our morning goals. The otherwise therapeutic progression of meditation, exercise and breakfast are routinely disrupted by bursts of passionate screaming, craftwork chaos, and unbridled toy-envy. We try our best to be respectfully attentive during these unanticipated inserts into our morning routine; trying to measure the style of our responsiveness in a way that complements the way we want to lead our lives in general: mindful, reflective, loving and forward-thinking.

It's all well and good, however, until it dawns on me that my child hasn't seen fit to embrace the same wavelength that I have. After all, *the scissors are clearly not working!* Before long, I find myself blurting out something that may as well be interpreted along the lines of "why can't you just be mindful and contemplative about this like I am?!"

But seriously, If I can say anything about my experiences both as a husband and as a father, I would sum it up with one word.

Shift.

While I cannot pretend to have 'figured out' parenthood by any stretch of the imagination, I can honestly attest to the fact that the father I am today is light years away from the father I first started out to be. While I feign to presume any 'arrival,' however, in the sense of having reached all the answers, this evolution in my ability to roll with the tide of family dynamics has been the result of a myriad shifts in my thinking and in my decisions to apply new learning. I sincerely take to heart Michel de Montaigne's sober caution that *"on the highest throne in the world, we still sit only on our own bottom,"* and therefore I do not presume to have "arrived" in any sense of the word. Much of my learning was at the cost of some very painful failures, though they nevertheless led to some positive turns at the same time.

18

Indeed, I have spent plenty of time looking back over the early years of my fatherhood with an uncomfortable degree of pain and regret over having not been what my children truly needed. Thankfully, it reached a point where I finally realized that even the arduous process of looking back itself was getting to be too much of a distraction, and that the primary sufferers of this perpetual mourning period, ironically, were my own children.

In a world where we are so caught up in our personal stories (and by extension, our so-called identities) we consequently form these crystallized conceptions of who we think we are. Added to this problem is the unfortunate social tendency of seeing ourselves through the lens of how we perceive others to see us. Consequently, we end up getting torn in this crazy tug-of-war between two perceptions, when the fact is that both of these negative images are being conjured up in the very same moment that we are entertaining them in our mind!

Yet beneath this decidedly sorry and sordid magician's act lies a much greater, though hidden, truth. This truth stipulates that every single thing which happens to us in our life is not the "me" of our fullest selves; it's simply an event. It's an experience. And while we may sometimes have an awful lot of the same experience over the course of our lives, it is still only that; a thing that informs us, yet is not the essential "us" in the deepest sense.

This is why we create misleading stories about ourselves. One of the biggest learned behaviors among our species is how we live according to the stories that we create. They dictate our behaviors, and they give justification to our most dogmatic beliefs.

Some years ago I was working with a client who was struggling considerably with knowing how to show intimacy to his wife. He loved his wife very much, yet somehow could not seem to find a way to get over this unfortunate block he had built up in his mind. It was a persona, a very specific belief about himself; a negative self-assessment that was preventing him from properly and healthfully translating his feelings for his wife into honest, physical affection. Part of his problem, it seemed, was that somewhere along the course of this relationship he had allowed the insecurities of his own childhood to creep in and distort everything that was happening in the present. This man told me about the various ways in which, as a child, he struggled to secure a basic sense of maternal stability from his mother – a woman who, I'm told, was quite preoccupied in her own struggles with mental illness.

As it turns out, this young man's difficulty in establishing a healthy, adult connection with his own wife became tragically marred by the context of what he had been unable to secure as a child. At the risk of sounding somewhat Freudian here, this is a familiar synopsis that many of us are probably aware of. Chances are that you could easily point to some man or woman in your own world whose current dysfunctions as a spouse are likely rooted in an earlier complication with their own father and mother.

Yet what was interesting about this particular young man in question was the story that he seemed so fixated on; the story which, ironically enough, was serving to sustain the very same problem he hated so much. He told me that, when it comes to showing affection to his wife, he envisions his wife as the most elegant, beautifully-crafted violin that he has the most longing desire to play, yet finds himself fumbling hopelessly with the bow. In other words, he tells himself that he is so terrified to even pick up the bow because he is so sure that he will make a horrible noise if he applies it to the violin. As such, he conveniently never picks up the bow.

Another analogy he liked to use was the idea that he sees himself as "a six-cylinder engine running on only four cylinders."

The telling part of this encounter, however, was in hearing his wife's side of the story. According to her, all she wanted was for him to freely just touch her, without thinking about it, and certainly without planning it. She didn't need to be "played," as he so fervently believed to be the case. She just needed to be loved and held. She just needed *him*.

I could tell by the way he portrayed his problem that he had obviously spent a long time ruminating on it, recycling it, and rehashing it until it had basically become embossed on his permanent psyche. His description of the "problem" was by no means a revelation in our counseling session. It was a carefully and faithfully recorded script that he had sold himself, and was now unconsciously doing everything in his power to sustain (even though it was the opposite of his heart's true desire). His story essentially became that he was a man who could not give his wife what he wanted to give her because of the distorted assumption that he was a disabled husband. Consequently, every time he

21

told himself the familiar violin story (a story which he had become very attached to) he was simply reinforcing his own negative beliefs. He was telling the story to himself repeatedly, just so that he wouldn't forget how disabled he really was.

Many of us have stories about ourselves. Despite how disturbing some of them might be, they have the wily ability to give definition to our private worlds in such a way that we feel we can recognize. We're so desperate for definition, and the critical disaster that we can sometimes end up living with is the personal identification with life's events rather than simply growing from them.

Additionally, the cold hard truth is that it's sometimes so much easier living with our problems than actually doing the work that it takes to overcome them.

The other important point here is that *events* and *circumstances* have a very gremlin-like knack of encroaching upon our sense of who we actually are at our core being, and we usually end up buying into the emotional baggage of these things with currency that we don't really have. It's like we're paying for a house that's really not right for us with credit that we are not good for. Consequently, we're left with this awful house that turns out to be haunted, yet we're too attached to it to even consider looking for the home that truly is where we belong. "Yeah, there's that freakish moaning sound that we always hear in the dining room, and there's the creepy-looking little boy in the rocking chair…but the house is on a really good street, and there's a decent school two blocks away for the kids."

When you think of it that way, it's really quite stupid. I mean, with all due respect, if that's how I'm thinking then maybe I actually *deserve* to live in a house filled with spooks. Yet, surprising as it may seem, so often we buy into a limiting story because of a certain set of temporary circumstances and, as a result, we neglect to consider other possibilities; other realities that are just as available.

The other insidious thing about stories is the way in which they dictate to us what the *future* stories in our life should look like as well, in addition to the ones we are already buying into. Based on pre-programmed data (that is, information which was originally intended as a learning tool but then unfortunately became crystallized into who we think we actually are, or are apparently supposed to be) we devise a set of future circumstances and aspirations that resemble and match our false sense of self.

True, these may be attractive things that we envision for ourselves. I mean, it's not like we're going to deliberately plan to have awful, diseased lives where we're feeling horrendously miserable and sickly. Naturally, we will seek to enjoy life as much as we possibly can while also engaging in a type of occupation or vocation that seems worthwhile to us. Yet the problem we can sometimes face is when we look at that future scenario with such an unmovable and inflexible gaze that we fail to notice (and take cue) from the subtle nuances that are intended to steer us in directions that we otherwise did not consider (usually much better directions, I might add). It's one thing to have a healthy vision about life. It's a whole other thing to write a rigid script for yourself that you're not willing to submit for adaptation to a higher Source.

All of these things come from the realm of personal belief. The stories we find ourselves in are based purely on beliefs that we chose to endorse somewhere along the path of our maturity. And like I already said, these beliefs are really based on events and situations that we chose to internalize rather than simply learn from.

In short, we picked up the baggage along the way of our journey through life, instead of simply observing the significance of what they had to teach us, and then just move on afterwards.

The *art*, as it were, is to somehow move through the events in life while resisting the temptation to invest too much in them, or to purchase illegitimate stock in them.

There is a true and noble process of life. The success of this process is found through being honestly informed by every curve and pitfall that comes to us, yet not allowing any of these things to dictate our limitations along the way. Indeed, some of life's worst circumstances will cross our path for the express purpose of forging a better resilience, or a greater ability to appreciate the sheer beauty of mystery. The ultimate martial art is to resist the cold realm of fixation in our lives and to roll majestically with the unknown, all the while trusting that your greater self is being exercised in the process.

I wish to emphasize here that answers will come to you when you simply decide to sit with yourself quietly, and face your strange stories. Without a doubt, only *you* can facilitate the honest transformation and rebranding of these stories. Only *you* can let them go.

As a case in point, here's one of my stories…

Playing House

Growing up, I had very few distinctive ideas about what I wanted to do in life, or what I wanted to become. But what I did know beyond any reasonable doubt, however, was that I wanted to be a father. I had grown up with some very specific ideals about what it meant to be a parent, as well as what it meant to be a child. There was a very discernible structure to these roles, and in my own household while growing up there was little room for debate or questioning on the matter. Some of it was honorable, but some of it was also quite ill-advised and forged through circumstances of religious fear and insecurity.

But I didn't just want to be any father, mind you. I wanted to be the absolute best father I could possibly be. I wanted to be Superdad. To me, successful fatherhood had always been the barometer of human worth itself; the threshold between human integrity and human dysfunction. As far as I was concerned, being a good father was the one distinction that could rescue a man from all the other failures he may endure over his lifetime, and reserve him a dignified place at the table of honorable humanity. This perception aside, I personally never doubted my potential to be an excellent father. Indeed, it was the one thing I always believed I could really be.

For many years my imaginations were vivid with images of being the special confidante for my developing child, the anchor of strength for his or her distresses, the 'weaver of words' for their unspoken ailments, and the dispenser of healing wisdom for their occasional wounds as they gradually tested the waters of their social environment with ever-guarded trepidation. I saw myself as the hero in their story; the knight who rescues at a moment's notice, armed with a mystical form of confidence and assurance. Basically, I just saw myself as an awesome dad, all around. A domestic guru-warrior-yogi, if you will.

Clearly, I saw something that I could be. Even as a very young teen, this is what I imagined. If I wasn't thinking specifically of the role itself, I often found myself conjuring up images of tasks and activities that were associated with being a father and husband. I would see myself driving to work, and coming home again to a house of bustling noise and activity. I would see myself filling the grocery cart with various items that reflected a house full of children. I could even hear myself referring to "my wife," or "my kids" in staged, imagined conversations with future co-workers and people I would meet in public. It was no stretch for me whatsoever to speculate on the sense of pride and satisfaction I would have in being able to refer to these very special people in my life; to talk about them freely and to be able to thrive in the experience of simply just having them in my home.

But then something happened to change all of that.

My first child was born.

My first recollection of falling short of this Father-Knows-Best picture I had illustrated for myself was while we were still in the hospital, shortly after his birth. Our son Asher came to us a couple of weeks ahead of 'schedule' and, as such, I felt grossly unprepared.

Without going too intimately into these details, suffice it to say that I had many expectations of what the "story" of early family should look like. As such, there was no room in this story for chronic illness, emergency cesarean sections, neonatal intensive care units, looming deadlines in college and copious financial struggle. Yet it was all there, grinning at us in the face and inviting us step boldly into the water of the unknown.

I can see how my own personal ideals and fantasies of fatherhood were pretty much destined to meet the pavement of how life actually tends to unfold sometimes. For me, facing reality was not a very welcome thing and I know that I tried to resist it on a number of occasions. At the end, however, it was all I could do to just accept certain things and try to move forward with some of my ideals broken, yet my integrity relatively still intact.

Unfortunately for our first child, however, it would mean his start in life was be impacted by some of the cleansing I would need to go through not merely as a father, but as an overall human being who had his own agenda of how the world should look and operate. Consequently, what would later unfold in Asher's life would become, as best as I can describe it, a very challenging and bumpy road of learning, failing, and overall pioneering in a territory of parenthood that I really knew nothing about – and would have to learn from the ground up.

The interesting thing is that I thought I knew the path before I even started. I thought I had the answers before the questions were even presented. For so many years I prided myself on having a knowledge of the contours of human society, yet this was about to be shattered in pieces – primarily because my own beliefs on parenthood had just started to fall apart, within moments of actually becoming a parent.

Essentially, the early months of my son's life were very difficult for me. In fact, I look back on that period as perhaps standing out as one of the most challenging experiences of my life, principally because I had no idea that I was being held hostage by my own self-derived fantasy; a fantasy which – although clearly being exposed as illegitimate – was still looming nakedly in my psyche.

The concept of paternal postpartum depression has been studied by researchers for at least the last two decades, though not to an exhaustive degree. Those who have examined it in depth, however, have discovered that issues of relationship dissatisfaction, lack of spousal support, absence of community involvement and even generation-gap era parenting (ie. fathers who were raised in the 70's and 80's) are among some of the more tangible factors that can lead to paternal postpartum depression (or PPD for short). A popular meta-analysis in 2010 by researchers Paulson and Bazemore looked at 43 separate studies from 16 different countries, and ultimately found a PPD rate of 10.4% among the overall population. Consequently, advocates of this area of study have been pressing for the need to recognize it as a substantial mental health concern that is especially unique to our modern epoch of the parenting culture.

For myself, I really can't say whether what I was experiencing was 'paternal postpartum depression' at the time of my first child's birth and beyond, but I feel fairly certain that - whatever it was – it lasted for a lengthy period and inevitably affected my ability to be fully present with him at the best of times. Not to say that I was an absentee father or that I had no time for him, however. On the contrary, I took my role as a father very seriously, and ended up endorsing an agonizing degree of pain and remorse over not being able to attend to my son in the way that I fundamentally believed I should be.

In truth, being unable to deliver on my ideals as a parent was killing me, specifically because I wanted to give so much of what was in me to give, yet for some reason I could not seem to find the means to translate this into an actual relationship exchange. Instead, our unfolding dynamic as a father and son became earmarked with fits of yelling at each other, mutual accusations, shaming and periodic spanking (every single one of which I regretted, by the way). Subsequently, I experienced the early years of my son's life as an exhausted, emotionally-depleted father.

The most crippling aspect of these earlier years was the way in which my personal identification with failure served to reinforce some dysfunctional elements in my own parenting. In that sense, I wasn't living with difficult children. I was living with the incessant weight of a difficult self-concept. A concept that I had bought into simply because I was categorically unable to face realities and circumstances that were alternative to the carefully-crafted image I had conceived of as a young man without children.

To put it plainly, I had a preconception of how family life should function, and once those preconceptions were threatened or challenged, I ended up interpreting those things as personal injuries. As a result, I was left with two struggles: the ongoing irritation of a new reality, and the overpowering sensation of a failed story in the face of it all. Translation: a failed *parent*.

> *"Peace begins when expectation ends."* – Sri Chinmoy

I can say with all honesty that the essential shift in my perspective came through the singular act of permitting myself the freedom to simply go back to square one. Back to the drawing board of life, you could say. My ability to move forward into better alignment with life itself was through finally letting go of whatever fictionalized scenarios I had anticipated taking place prior to becoming a parent (many of which, you could argue, were nothing more than a stroking of my own ego), and to regard with new and unfettered eyes the truth of the real moment I was finding myself in.

Over time I have gained enough self-transparency to be able to at least recognize that any change in my well-practiced trend of ego-disappointment needed to begin with me. I simply had to accept the very likely possibility that I was the chief instigator of these difficulties that had been plaguing me for so long, and that any hope of becoming an accessible father would ultimately depend on whatever I could change about myself in the few short years that were left of my kids' childhood. Whether I was owning too much guilt or not was beside the point. The simple fact was that I could no longer wait in vain for my child to 'see reason' in these discourses. I basically had to take some solid leadership in this arena. I had to accept full responsibility, once and for all, and place zero expectation on any other being, apart for myself.

I was, after all, my children's father.

I'll just conclude this entry by pointing out that I'm clearly not there yet. I'm still learning this whole parenting thing, and am doing my utmost to be alert to any skewed perceptions or distortions in my thinking that may serve to imbalance my effectiveness in simply being present with my children. The other difficult part in this whole exercise is to resist the temptation to over-analyze or deconstruct, ad nauseam, my relationship with my kids. I don't want to treat my children like a science experiment, nor do I want to make them the subject of some narcissistic theater of my own life.

My story is, in many ways, a contradiction of two worlds. While I am driven by the compulsion and the belief that reality can be changed and impacted by our own actions, I am also faced on a nearly-daily basis with the fact that I cannot simply 'imagine' an alternative universe or reality that other people are living in – particularly my own family members. To some degree, I have to own a heavy measure of responsibility in responding to the facts of what already exists – and I am likewise accountable for illegitimate actions that I may have once committed, though since forgotten. In consequence, this plays into my relationship with my children on so many levels; affecting the finest, most subtle, aspects of my interacting with them.

My story is a personal one, like that of every other person out there. But I feel that it's important to share simply because of the profound way that it has touched the development of my children, for better or for worse. After all, my children will be interacting with your children at some point in our future as we move collectively forward as a race, and if there is anything I can share about this journey that will be a help or an inspiration to others out there, that would be so worth it for me.

Now, speaking of our children…

3

Awakening to What Is

"It was the best of times, it was the worst of times, it was the age of wisdom, it was the age of foolishness, it was the epoch of belief, it was the epoch of incredulity, it was the season of Light, it was the season of Darkness, it was the spring of hope, it was the winter of despair, we had everything before us, we had nothing before us, we were all going direct to Heaven, we were all going direct the other way…"

- A Tale of Two Cities

So begins Dickens' legendary portrayal of the societal turbulence and unrest that led to the French Revolution. In these few poetic words, the writer unveils what we might today perceive to be a poignant reflection of where our hearts and minds are currently sitting in the modern epoch of Western living; an age where our unprecedented social affluence overlaps with our shared sense of poverty and scarcity, and the mettle of our deepest values are being increasingly tested against the aggressive edges of economic and social unrest (or perhaps social *media* unrest).

One would have to agree that, today, we are endowed with such an exacerbated degree of material convenience in our lives that we truly do live as kings and queens – regardless of the fact that our global economic resources are still so tragically disproportionate in other parts of the world. For the majority of us in the West, we continue to enjoy the fruits of our labor in ways that contrast sharply from previous eras in history and, try as hard as we can, we struggle to identify with the level of deprivation and corruption that is so graphically obvious for millions of other people on the planet.

Within the midst of this season of our enjoyment, however, lies a concerning reality which, although perhaps having forever been a plague to our hearts since the inception of humanity, is probably far more distinctive right now than it ever has before. What I am referring to here is the integrity of our conscious connection with each other as global citizens.

The Need for Awakening

In some senses, perhaps, it can be regarded as a very good thing that we find ourselves in such a loud era of social narcissism, painfully extroverted media content and manic entrepreneurial angst, since it is by the merit of such stark contrast that the deeper riches of thoughtful service and contemplative regard can be more vividly seen for the rare gems they are. In this sense, the unrelenting noise of our social surroundings may actually serve as the historical catalyst we need in this very moment in order to narrow our eyes on the more critical aspects of what it means to be a human *being*, rather than a human *reacting*, or a human *consuming*.

Specifically, it can be said that we are at a crossroads in terms of the development of our collective consciousness, and the dilemma of this is felt in its purest sense within the private and intimate domain of the human mind. Today, arguably more potent than eras gone by, our mind is being incessantly stimulated and worn out by an endless stream of thoughts and distractions; most of which can be classified as either pursuits of entertainment or the response to social pressures. It goes without saying that the digital boom has been a huge contributor of this state of affairs.

Deep down inside each of us, however, is the realization that this incessant and loud pulling at the strings of our weary brains is not how life should really be. We want meaning in our life, yet we also cannot avoid the pungent possibility that our image or even our affluence may be at risk if we 'bow out of the race' of our peers, so to speak. We also don't want to be cogs in some mass, mechanized system, yet we're similarly at a loss as to how to exist outside of that paradigm either. We just don't know how to *be* the person we are aspiring to be while being hit by all the other thousand things in life, most of which, we already understand, are really not that important.

Martin Heidegger, the 20th century German philosopher underscored the interesting concept of *dasein* or, in English, "being there." In its most basic application, dasein simply refers to the idea that our sense of being is manifested and cultivated as a result of our proximity with other humans. It specifically implies that our humanity is formed through the myriad, complex exchanges and relationship dynamics that play out within the social tapestry of the overall population. Naturally, this stands in direct contrast with the popular Cartesian view that we are fundamentally separate, individualistic beings whose true identity and "core" can only be seen in isolation from other beings. In some senses, this concept of dasein departs quite sharply from the otherwise traditional views of individualism, mostly because of its emphasis on how a person's overall sense of place in the world (or the universe) is a direct product of their being intimately woven into the fabric of other people's lives and experiences.

In other words, what we perceive to be our individual and private worlds are really only personalized experiences within a much wider, organic and pulsating collective. We are creatures that have significance not through separation from the population, but rather through the inherent role of 'being there,' in the midst of what we might popularly call the "other." As far as dasein is concerned, the self and the other are mutually intractable things that are really playing out a very intimate dance which – by its very phenomenon – generates the whole essence of being human.

Insofar as the personal consciousness is concerned, it seems that the dasein argument would imply that – by necessary extension – the individual consciousness is also connected *to* and influenced *by* the consciousness of every other human being. The idea that we are connected in such intimate ways (including the even more important *subconscious* connection we share) suggests that our task in cultivating a healthy, spiritual consciousness for ourselves has very critical implications for other people.

The challenge we face at the personal level is that our spiritual development is so easily distracted and influenced because of the "dance," so to speak. The very existence of this phenomenon does not imply either bad or good, necessarily, but simply just that – a phenomenon that we are wise to be aware of, in order that we may use the dance to our advantage and train our subconscious in such a way that is healthy and free. Otherwise, we are so quickly swept up in the tide of so many collective energies, many of which are based on widely-held beliefs that engender fear and distrust about life itself.

By a necessary extension, this personal dilemma is sometimes vividly experienced and played out in the intimate dynamic of our own families. It is felt between spouses, and it finds expression in the intimate relationship between the parent and their child. In this way, we can say that a conscious, spiritual revolution is sitting at our doorstep, and that the consequences of this tension depend on how we choose to meet these challenges in our own personal season of life, particularly in our families.

Such a challenge compels us to be awakened as human beings, especially since one of the greatest gifts you can give your child is the awakened you.

The incessant hum of functional addiction

Raising children is one of the oldest professions in the world. While we have an indecipherable number of years of human progression in the wisdom of harvesting young children into socially and spiritually-conscious people, the uncomfortable truth remains that this progression has become dramatically interrupted by some fairly drastic changes that have popped up in society over the last few years.

It goes without saying that the subject of mental wellbeing in our children is a hot topic in our culture, if not already cooled down by its ad nauseam exposure from which we have had an abundance of pharmacological reactions. While the concern of "screen time" also continues to be debated in the field of developmental psychology, one cannot ignore the fact that our virtual explosion of digital media today is running a paralleled course with rising levels of adverse mental health symptoms in our children; most notably the early onsets of both depression and anxiety.

In the June 2013 issue of the *European Journal of Public Health*, researchers Yang, Helgason, Sigfusdottir and Kristjansson discussed their findings of how adverse mental health symptoms correlated with excessive digital screen time (among 10-12 year-old children, in particular). The specific indicators they were looking for in their study included limited interest in activities, decreased appetite, loneliness, crying easily or the feeling of wanting to cry, difficulties with falling asleep or staying asleep, feelings of sadness, and feelings of hopelessness about the future.

As the researchers inevitably observed,

> "...findings consistently show that the odds of having experienced any of the negative symptoms sometime or often during the past 7 days increase with greater amount of time spent in front of electronic screens among both girls and boys"
> (p. 494).

The fact is that we are in an interesting epoch of progress whereby our intellectual prowess often seems to be outrunning our capacity for mindfully and quietly observing the path in which it's taking. We're so caught up in the act of keeping up with the curve that we seldom stop to consider if there are better, healthier ways of engaging with our environment than through media and the latest technology. In so doing, we sometimes fool ourselves by thinking that we're always going to be responsibly managing the onslaught of digital accessibility in our world today, let alone mythologizing that our children can somehow handle it. Yet this addiction has become our norm, and any effort to mitigate its influence in our lives is met with such intellectual resistance that we simply cannot make the changes that we inherently, somehow, deep down inside, feel that we need to make.

These are the changes that our *children* need us to make.

I am no enemy to technological advances, mind you. They have their place in our lives, and it is evident that they have provided innumerable benefits in a variety of ways. Our digital advances have opened the door to myriad entrepreneurial and social opportunities, even providing outlets for disenfranchised and oppressed populations to be able to torpedo their perspectives out into the social stratosphere – effectively resulting in much-needed change in their specific geopolitical milieu. I do get this. Furthermore, I would never want to stand in the way of honorable research in the areas of modern medicine, clean energy and environmental sustainability. To a large extent, these are arenas that affect each of us in very significant ways, and will perhaps become more so for future generations.

For our families, however, the reality is such that we live in social climates whereby our availability to our children (and our spouses for that matter) is caught in a merciless state of competition with outside influences and vices. And while digital technology is not the sole agent responsible for this, it is probably one of the most obvious and visible ones affecting our current era. I mean, do we really need our neocortex to be uploaded to the cloud? Is that not something we surely can do without?

A mantra we hear over and over again is that of the distracted person who asserts the need to not be quite so distracted in life. 'Moderation' is the aspired goal in such contexts, and we somehow placate our guilt over these addictions to distractions by chanting the well-worn anthem that we are doing our best to try and minimize the role of these things in our lives. In fact, this has become such a routine way of living that we have essentially built an entire industry around the concept of minimizing; of making things 'easier' in order to survive the sheer tidal wave of distractions that bombard us at every turn. As such, we are drawn towards convenience in our lives, of strategies and products that render the complicated as uncomplicated as possible, and that purchase us more time for the things in life that are more important to us. We learn to maximize the easy things so that we can minimize the hard things.

But what happens when we begin to view the complexities of family life as one of the 'hard things?' What happens when the necessary and fundamental complications of raising an individualistic child (or two or three of them, for that matter) reaches a point where it becomes acceptable to us to make certain sacrifices in attending to their deeper, more complex needs for the sake of simply getting through the day and having the bills paid?

For that matter, when are things made convenient just enough, so that nothing further is needed?

My underlying question here is this: have we allowed ourselves to graduate to such a point of manipulating our natural household culture where we simply cannot receive the genuine, organic flow of life in its most authentic textures and colors? Do we upload our children to the *cloud*, so to speak, instead of helping them find their proper footing on the earth?

Contrary to the practice of taking away, or eliminating specific things in our life (such as distractions or unwanted complexities) the art of *receiving* invokes the concept of simply accepting a thing for what it is. Nothing more, nothing less. This is the idea that a thing appears in our life for a reason, and with that appearing comes the opportunity to either learn something pivotal or to instead dismiss it as something that needs to be eliminated. This is true for every individual, and not just the busy parent.

Our limbic system has become well-primed for sensing discomfort or danger in the face of certain situations, and so it is naturally quite typical for the modern person to view uncertain or unfamiliar events as somewhat suspect. In addition, we are now programmed to be so divided and strained in our professional workplaces that we automatically cancel out or discredit, in an instant's notice, anything that does not appear to be immediately crucial for our brain to consider. Without realizing it, we scan our environment with artillery speed and we make lightning decisions simply due to the bombardment of too many stimulants and too many details that would otherwise consume us. We've become highly proficient at quickly rooting out the most relevant information within dramatically quick successions of time, and this practice is further reinforced by the fact that it is being increasingly rewarded in the workplace. In some senses, it has come to be seen as a skill, rather than the potentially moral defect that it sometimes can be. This is because, in due course of time, our 'expert' performance in our workaday lives can easily steal the greater parts of who we are, subsequently leaving us with very little to give our spouses and our children when we return to them. Often we come to this place simply because we thought we were being economical about our commitments. We thought we were doing the responsible thing, merely because society told us that this was the right and normal arrangement of things.

It's rather ironic, then, that we assumed we've been making the simpler choices when, in fact, our practical methodology for mapping out our lives has served to overcomplicate the natural, quiet wonder of our personal and family development, rather than actually feed it in the way that it needs. And when family life begins to steer a moral course that is governed by the sheer stress of living according to such standards meted out by others, we start to lose focus. And quickly.

Yet, at any moment, we can heed the call to open our eyes to fuller living. As it is with any other natural and authentic surge of human growth, it begins in a mindful state.

More than just a buzzword

Mindfulness is the act (or the art, rather) of being attentive to the present, as opposed to the past or the future, both of which, arguably, do not even exist. In a mindful state, an individual is able to appreciate that they are not the same entity as their mere thoughts. Rather, they become the unthreatened observer of those thoughts. In the mindful state, the individual no longer has to judge the thoughts or emotions that come to the surface of their consciousness, but instead simply accepts them and regards them for what they are without the burden of being distracted by them.

Mindfulness means accepting the moment, the present, without any effort of pushing or forcing unwanted thoughts aside. In this way, mindfulness essentially releases us to the art of experiencing life rather than fearing it, dreading it, regretting it, or wishing it was happening in some other form. It's no surprise, then, that mindfulness can often be regarded as synonymous with meditation.

Meditation, for that matter, is an ancient practice which has long since served to still the mind and facilitate higher evolution of thought and wisdom. Today, our scientific discoveries have revealed that such mindful states play a central role in the calming and inhibiting of our amygdala, which is the storehouse for our emotional memories and the trigger for our fight, flight and freeze responses. Furthermore, meditation has also been shown to stimulate our left prefrontal cortex (the part of the brain associated with pleasure and feelings of peace). As Khusid and Vythilingam (2016) point out, *"meditation changes the relationship to negative thoughts by making one more aware, yet more open and accepting of negative experiences, thereby decreasing their intensity"* (p. 963).

To be sure, mindfulness, while at one time found primarily in closely-knit spiritual communities scattered throughout the world, is now being experienced in increasing measures across multiple societies and cultures. Perhaps its most fascinating emergence has been in the Western world over the last little sliver of our history, arguably because of the way that it stands out with such great contrast from the rest of our manic, "crush it"- oriented society.

While there could be many reasons for this relatively new appearance of it, I think that there are two specific things that have led to the way in which mindfulness has reached such widespread popularity – particularly its Western variation.

The first reason would simply be associated with the spiritual shift that began materializing during the earlier part of the 20th century; perhaps most notably marked by such yogic trailblazers like Paramhansa Yogananda, Swami Vivekananda, Jiddu Krishnamurti and several others. These historic figures played an unprecedented role in the migration of Vedic wisdom into the Western hemisphere – as well as the initial introduction of original yoga and related meditation practices. Interestingly, in his book *American Veda*, author Philip Goldberg identifies an even earlier transmission of these spiritual themes through the writings of Ralph Waldo Emerson, Henry David Thoreau and Walt Whitman –

specifically due to their being among the earliest
Americans to have been exposed to English translations
of Vedic literature, with the subsequent essence of such
things having bled into their own influential writings.
So in some senses, you could say that early American
literature was not without its Eastern influences.

Consequently, over the last two centuries many people
have gradually begun to identify a decisive line between
spirituality and religion; pointing out that these are often
two very different themes and should therefore not
always be confused with each other. Simultaneously, as
we move even further into a post-feminist culture, with
the subsequent waves of social awareness having been
mercilessly thrust upon the archaic conventions of
religion and many of its inflexible, patriarchal
associations, spirituality itself has ultimately begun
experiencing a new birth, for lack of a better term. A
new incarnation, even.

It's become all but redundant in today's world to make
the distinction that one is "spiritual but not religious."
In fact, the very application of a religious label today can
sometimes even be seen as an insult, resulting in the
terse assertion that one is not in the least bit religious,
thank you very much. With the added phenomenon
that even the atheist can now ascribe a form of
'spirituality' to him or herself that is void of any form of
Higher Intelligence whatsoever, we are essentially left
with a society in which spirituality – as a concept - has
become more deeply rooted into our collective human
psyche. If anything, we have reached a stage of social
understanding in which spirituality is commonly being
understood as an entrenched aspect of our humanity,
and not necessarily something that we formally need to

sign up for or commit ourselves to. It is simply there in our behavioral makeup, whether we have a religious background or not.

To this effect, mindfulness is now being seen simply as a way of being. And while it is often referred to as a 'spiritual' act, it is granted an existence that does not have to be exclusively perceived as being connected to the concept of God or 'Spirit,' necessarily, and can actually be adopted as a decidedly secular enterprise altogether. It is seen as a pre-existing part of our organic composition that can be nurtured, developed, and mastered – just like any other part of our humanity. In addition, because we are becoming ever more aware of the fact that mindfulness is harvested through a practice of inner reflectivity - as well as a deeply-rooted awareness of wisdom and knowledge which, apparently, is not so external to us as we once thought - the thought of a literal 'God' figure becomes less and less necessary to our wellbeing (as some would conclude).

With this in mind, I think it can be reasonable to say that to be 'spiritual' is to basically underscore the fact that we are truly the human beings of a modern epoch. Regardless of any particular moral ascriptions (since one man's spirituality can be another man's hell), spirituality is increasingly being regarded as a "how" of being, and not so much the "what" of it. In his famous book *Franny and Zooey*, J.D. Salinger's portrayal of Zooey – a heavily cynical, acid-tongued, culturally-deviant young adult – reveals a stunning experience of spiritual awareness that takes the reader quite by surprise. As we gradually get to know the character, we also see a fascinating picture of awareness that emerges in the face of his tortured attempts to navigate the dysfunctions of his own family, choice of education and the questionable meaning of his career. While Salinger's book has clearly been the subject of much attention and debate as to its specific message, I personally see the story as a portrayal of ancient wisdom finally merging with the modern world, and the clash that naturally comes out as a result - yet ultimately yielding to a higher awareness of our place in the universe and our continued efforts to move forward in a very urgent world using ancient knowledge as our primary compass.

A second reason that mindfulness has rocketed itself into mainstream culture probably has a lot to do with the pioneering work of Dr. Jon Kabat-Zinn and his development of Mindfulness-based Stress Reduction (MBSR) in the 1970's. Kabat-Zinn's work basically broke a substantial hole in the overly-crustified mainframe of psychotherapeutic treatment of the time, taking the incredible leap of introducing ancient Buddhist meditation techniques into Western-based treatment modalities. This gave rise to a wholesale movement in mainstream practice where more and more therapeutic professionals began incorporating the simple prescription of mindfulness into their work with clients, which inevitably led to a plethora of peer-reviewed studies that have given considerable praise to the profound power of mindfulness-based strategies in combating depression, anxiety and PTSD, among other things. Active clinical research continues today in the academic world, partly because our society has grown very fascinated by this strange "new" discovery.

One of the interesting aspects of this newly-embraced cultural treasure of mindfulness is the way in which it has opened the door for a new expression of spirituality. Essentially, the last few decades of scientific and religious progression have allowed for an ancient Buddhist influence to pave the way for a new way of looking at the universe, and specifically at our personal lives within the greater context of that universe. As such, new ground has been broken in terms of asking more profound questions about ourselves, ultimately turning our attention to the inner world of our own private thought process as opposed to the external, theoretical world that has traditionally been defined by doctrine, creed and community.

Interestingly, however, the Judeo-Christian philosophies that have been so prevalent in the West – when traced back to their earliest roots in the Torah writings – actually did not even begin with a focus on religious doctrine. In fact, when one undertakes a meditative review of Jewish sacred texts, one finds that the insights contained in those writings have much more to do with the mystical journey of self-mastery than the concept of structured worship. As it happened, however, what began as a sacred prescription for successful living eventually devolved into a vast subset of organized observances that took on many lives and cultures of their own, over time. Coincidentally, this devolution continued to unfold throughout history to a point where, today, people are recognizing something more freeing and decidedly liberating about Eastern spirituality that has been otherwise squeezed out of traditional Christian and Talmudic orientations.

In many senses, Jesus has met with the Buddha, yet Moses had been waiting for them in the quiet wilderness the whole time. But contrary to most of the buzz surrounding mindfulness today, however, being 'awakened' is only a starting point in our journey.

Awakening is merely the beginning

"I have awakened, I have really awakened and have just been born today." - Hermann Hesse

Awakening is just the start of our journey, and not the end. We can just as easily run the risk of allowing our own awakening to become a mere extension of our affluent selves, which naturally snuffs out any sense of being awakened in the first place. The moment someone assumes they have "arrived" is the very same moment that they can so easily be overtaken by the sleep of fools. This is why one of the primary impulses of this book is the conviction that we are brought into this world for human service and for the building up of our healthiest infrastructures. Because of this, a meaningful contemplation of life serves merely as the chief tool for necessary transformation and should not be mistaken as the final outcome. My personal perspective is that there really is a Divine Appointment for our species, and that we are being increasingly beckoned to step outside of our concrete and digital paradises in order to properly connect with it.

While many parents clearly have the desire to invest in their personal ability to find 'presence' in their daily lives, the whole concept of kids "stopping us from evolving" is a mythology that needs to be radically turned on its head. In many respects, I have become increasingly convinced that children can act as incredible catalysts for our evolution and soulful refinement, rather than serve as distractions from it. Life truly has a way of showing us many reasons why being present is so important, and how children, ironically, can serve to inform and inspire our personal journey to higher thinking and consciousness. In many ways, children serve as the key to this achievement, and not the barrier. As Ram Dass himself once indicated, every other person in our environment can become a guru to us once we lay aside our ego and release ourselves to the joy of being transformed. What greater guru, then, than the unscathed child who has not yet been overly-duped and drugged by this world's frantic enterprises? What greater mystical source of wisdom for our dilapidated selves than the child who has not bought into this world's manufactured systems in the same way we have?

Sounds crazy? Overly-optimistic? As many others have said, we often find ourselves in challenging situations that we struggle to navigate and understand. So we therefore have two choices: remove ourselves completely, or surrender to the dynamic of what truly is. With that in mind, one of the aims of this book is to underscore the amazing possibilities that come through plunging one's self into the remarkable odyssey of raising children and allowing that very station itself to serve as a beautifully-dynamic sanctuary for essential transformation.

In some senses, parenting is the church. It's the synagogue, the mosque, the temple and the sanctuary. Immersion into the raw flux and flow of family life is essentially the pristine experience of a spiritual life, primarily because it is the ultimate holy place where our humanity is allowed to harvest and refine itself to an ever-expansive degree.

There's a reason why traditional monks and mystics go to remote monasteries for elongated experiences of inner peace and tranquility. And there is a place for this, absolutely. Yet the true practitioner of peace is one who is able to not only survive in the real world of conflict and distortion, but who can find liberation and lasting transformation in the very same heat of those things. This is because the real world offers us a well-disguised gift in its various forms of stressors and detailed imperfections. The ability, therefore, to train one's mind and spirit to move steadily forward in the face of so much neurological stimulus (whether good or bad) is what defines the truly peaceful martial artist, and it is this very ability that sets a person apart from the masses.

With that in mind, when the practitioner immerses him or herself into the willful art of being present with a child, it is then that the entire universe truly begins to open up.

4

The Jewel in the Fire

"I think the real miracle is not to walk either on water or in thin air, but to walk on earth."

- Thich Nhat Hahn

Patience is one of the greatest things I have struggled with as a parent. Ironically, I've been described as an extremely patient person by friends and co-workers for as long as I can remember. Yet, when it comes to actually being present with my own children, I have somehow found it difficult to maintain a patient disposition with them, even at the best of times.

I think part of this problem had a lot to do with personal exhaustion, to be honest with you. We're told that the "spirit is willing, but the flesh is weak," and it certainly comes to mind that, despite all of our efforts to approach the sensitivities of our children with a mindful framework, it can be too easy for a busy parent to digress into primal reactivity when we perceive our kids to be unreasonable, illogical…or even just really annoying.

While I'm told that fathers tend to struggle with this the most, I have certainly observed similar difficulties among mothers as well. While I'm not so sure that it's always been a historical issue, it's quite obvious that it is a contemporary one, especially in light of how divided our families are today and also when considering the fantastic pressures that are placed on young families in our current economy and doctrine-laden social structure. For myself, I can fully appreciate that my children need me to be accessible and available to them without cost, and my sincere desire is to provide that for each one of them. On the other hand, all of my best intentions are so frequently interrupted by a thousand other factors.

I sometimes speculate that if I were to be 100% available to my children at every instance of their childhood, I would probably never get a single thing done in life. Certainly, living in a modern culture that is devoid of the proverbial "village" of helpers and supporters, one is left to navigate and commandeer so many fine details of domestic life purely by themselves. And let's face it. No sensible person actually wants their house, their mental wellbeing and their livelihood to suffer in order to attend to every whim and panic that a child brings to them. Yet that is precisely how it feels sometimes when, in the throes of trying to manage a functioning household, our efforts are easily bypassed by the myriad grievances that our children seem plagued with. To us, our children's concerns and issues can seem so utterly trivial, so irrelevant in comparison with the crazy dance that we're trying to sort out as responsible adults in a disorienting, ever-shifting world. As a result, it's no surprise that we find ourselves reacting to these most vulnerable people in our life in ways that make us feel badly about ourselves afterwards.

We tell ourselves we're not going to yell at them again. We tell ourselves that next time we'll put more effort into actually hearing about their crises, or that we will just take the time to listen to their little story. We tell ourselves that we will finally just be a better parent. We also convince ourselves that we will forego the stance of 'instruction' and simply just bend down and meet our crying, angry, hurt child face to face, and just be with them. Yet somehow we falter again. And again.

In my observation, there are a couple of things going on here. In the first sense, natural attachment to another human being (such as a child to a parent) will necessarily involve a need for closeness, or for some degree of affirmation, or security. When this closeness is perceived to be at risk, however, or when it gets strained in some way, the child will either make heavier demands on the parent (which the parent will find even harder to accommodate), or the child will feel the need to draw back instead which, in its own way, can also serve as a stressor for the parent since this can often manifest in behavioral symptoms such as overt opposition. It can even be perceived as outright criticism or personal rejection toward the parent, which can be extremely hard to swallow when we are not feeling centered.

Yet I believe that our children's need for our accessibility is exactly on queue; that it is in no way a distortion of their developmental journey. Rather, it is *us* who have gotten so far behind in our ability to keep in step with *them*, to the point where their most natural needs and inquisitions are experienced in ways that seem overwhelming, taxing, and even invasive to us. Again, we can be very tired people sometimes, and our habitual programming is to reserve all the best parts of energies for things *outside* the realm of family (such as the professional world), and not the intricate and complex things within.

With these things in mind, are our children asking a lot from us? The answer, of course, is yes.

Similarly, do we sometimes address their needs in ways that are emotionally inappropriate or perhaps even neglectful at times? Again, the answer is yes.

So what do we do with this?

As a first point, we need to understand that guilt will only get us so far before it eventually serves a detrimental effect. We really need to be kind enough to ourselves to not get too hung up on guilt. While the pangs of guilt are natural and serve an educational purpose for us, it's when we start to dwell on the guilt itself that it starts to take on an illegitimate authority in our overall judgment as parents. The fact is that our child does not need us to be berating ourselves and beating ourselves up. While it may be helpful in generating a notable sense of humility (and perhaps even well-justified remorse at the odd time), it's not the same thing as actually learning and applying anything. Children benefit far more when their mother or father is simply able to reflect on the situation at hand, and to adjust themselves accordingly.

Think about when somebody causes you pain or severe discomfort. Are you genuinely satisfied to find out that all they've ended up doing afterwards is to harbor a lot of self-deprecating guilt about it? How does such a chronic response of personal regret in the other person actually serve you? Where is the contemplation, the learning, the adjusting of perspective and – more importantly – the disciplined efforts to re-evaluate and restore the relationship? This is why guilt can be an unusually insidious factor in relationship malfunction, particularly in the parent-child relationship.

When permitted to fester in the heart of the immature parent, guilt can create a massive gulf between both sides of the relationship, and it cancels out any possibility for a true meeting of the minds. This is because one side of the family equation – the parent – becomes so distracted by the sheer regret of the experience that they end up allowing it, inappropriately, to become associated with their distorted sense of identity. As mentioned earlier, the result is that the circumstance, or the event, becomes somehow fused into the person's very own persona rather than serving as an instructive signpost.

Naturally, there can be many different reasons why a mom or a dad will feel guilty. One of the big reasons parents end up feeling a lot of guilt is because of the impact in which pressures and commitments from their workplace end up colliding with their ability to be fully present and accessible to their child. In our current economy, this is almost universal. In the June 2017 issue of the *Journal of Child and Family Studies*, a team of researchers were able to confirm how parents' feelings of guilt can be largely correlated with high levels of work-family conflict, as well as long work hours in general. It was further shown how females tend to espouse feelings of guilt at a considerably higher rate than their male counterparts (Borelli et al., 2017).

While this is to be expected, given the natural, maternal response to a child's needs, it goes without saying that the men in our families are experiencing increasingly greater sensations of guilt as well – particularly as they try to orient themselves to the rapidly-changing landscape of social values and social expectations that are placed on young families today. In effect, it can be seen as a much harder task to maintain one's genuine individuality in the face of so much change, and the ability to stay quietly centered becomes even more challenged when dealing with the fuzzy, undefined demands of 21st century fatherhood.

Furthermore, there is a lot of discussion these days around the contrast between the highly-disciplined (or some might say abusive) techniques employed by our not-so-distant forebears and the decidedly softer approaches used by many parents in today's generation, and the obvious question of which one is more appropriate for the developing child. In his book *12 Rules for Life: An Antidote to Chaos*, psychologist and author Jordan Peterson reflects on the need for an intelligent balance in this regard, and the importance of recognizing both methods as unhealthy extremes.

"Children can be damaged as much or more by a lack of incisive attention as they are by abuse, mental and physical…(they) are damaged when those charged with their care, afraid of any conflict or upset, no longer dare to correct them, and leave them without guidance. I can recognize such children on the street. They are doughy and unfocused and vague. They are leaden and dull instead of golden and bright. They are uncarved blocks, trapped in a perpetual state of waiting-to-be" (Peterson, p. 122).

The problem ultimately lies in our personal sense of disorientation, fundamentally beginning within the realm of our own true selves. Personally speaking, my worst moments of fathering have been when my core values have become hopelessly confused while under the intoxicating influence of my social surroundings, and all of the diverging value systems that come along with it. These have been periods where, instead of being able to take thoughtful consideration of my deepest perspectives and insights, I instead allowed myself to become railroaded by the onslaught of surrounding information to the point of becoming altogether misinformed on what is truly right for me and for my house. Consequently, my decidedly schizophrenic-like detachment from my own insight has repeatedly led to situations at home where my connection with my children has been anything *but* connected.

Without a doubt, disconnect from the true self leads to disconnect from the child.

Once the guilt is then granted the opportunity to become rooted enough in our own self-identification, it can inevitably serve to offset the natural equilibrium that should otherwise be shared between parents and children. This is a dynamic which, when left unchecked, can distort a parent's ability to soberly provide authentic guidance and correction. Mostly, this is because of a strange sort of ambition that gets formed in which the parent mistakenly gropes for a kind of 'honeymoon-like' status with the child following an unpleasant confrontation. Basically, the parent ends up feeling that they need to make it up to the child, which often leads them to go the opposite extreme without any true, reflective learning. So we spoil our kids, we overindulge them, we distract them with meaningless entertainment and toys, and it's within the cunning space of this false romance that we actually feel like a healing has occurred. But then very soon afterwards we end up doubling-back to inappropriate behaviors towards them; demonstrating that no actual restorative learning ever really took place at all. All we really did was find a sweet moment of ceasefire in the midst of a more deeply-rooted history of conflict.

Past experience serves as one of our greatest teachers. Yet, previous faults and mistakes should never be regarded as "who" we are, but should instead serve as motivators for our current transition in life. Too many times we tell ourselves things like: "I'm that guy who screamed at my child," or "I'm the person who is causing so much pain in my kid's life," or "I am always doing this to my child." On the other hand, we're also guilty of labeling our child as the very source of our frustration. We emotionally appraise them as the perpetrator of our wounds when we say things like "you always do this to me," or "why do you have to be that way?" or "you just always have to be such a (*fill in the blank*)."

Between both of these extremes, however, lies a very special space which is largely unexplored in our modern culture. Despite our growing proximity with 'mindfulness' techniques, we remain grossly alienated from our children's natural energies by the very fact that we are perpetually alienated from our authentic selves, and excessively disconnected from who we truly are deep down inside. Furthermore, our former programming from earlier in life has – in many cases – led us to deal with our families from perspectives and stances that are largely social and ego-driven. In such cases, we revert to solution-focused methods of parenting which, although serving to some effect in mitigating certain tensions, ultimately leaves the problem of a much deeper disconnection relatively untouched.

True, most of us are becoming more and more aware of the basic tenets of mindfulness in today's arguably pro-Eastern cultural curve. As such, more people are turning to the yogic arts (ie. meditation practices and the like) as a way of finding some centering in their otherwise busy and hectic lives.

In some ways, however, our increasing attendance to mindfulness and meditation becomes an unexpected distraction for us on top of everything we're trying to stuff into our crazy lives. It becomes another 'thing' that we have to somehow fit in which, by that very same token, becomes another reason for our feeling threatened when the kids seem to be preventing us from actually practicing it! When we're not being careful about it, it's like we're blaming our kids for not letting us develop properly.

"Just leave me alone for 20 minutes so I can evolve!"

Without realizing the absurdity of it all, we can easily misappropriate mindfulness as a coping mechanism rather than as the transcending exercise that it actually is. This is because mindfulness, when responsibly practiced, begets a certain awakening in ourselves, and it is through this process that we are then able to shed the virtual layers of our false identities as well as our many self-imposed burdens and expectations.

A more thoughtful look at mindfulness

In its most pristine application, it means simply being in the now of the everyday, without having to exorcise one's physical self from the environment and all of its recurring discomforts. It's through this type of application that some of our most legendary leaders and historical figures were able to master their sense of personhood while being subject to unalterable circumstances such as imprisonment, isolation, or debilitating physical ailments.

In meeting Stephen Hawking for the very first time, an associate professor who spent some time at Cambridge University described how profoundly at peace this man was – despite the obvious limitations of his physical body. Hawking himself was famously quoted as saying that people *"need not be limited by physical handicaps as long as they are not disabled in spirit."*

While most of us may not experience the particular adversity of a chronic physical ailment necessarily, those who have walked such roads can sometimes be the most insightful among our species when it comes to giving wise prescription about difficulties in general. To this effect, Helen Keller once wrote that *"a happy life consists not in the absence, but in the mastery of hardships."*

The graphic texture of these experiences, in the lives of such influential figures we admire, was such that it impelled these individuals to transcend their immediate, sensual experience of the condition – though not the condition itself necessarily. It was through this form of inner transformation that the *condition*, in a sense, became the virtual temple or monastery, if you will, of their development. It obviously didn't feel very good at first, but that's the whole point. Transformation is often very difficult at first, and this is because we are so well-practiced at doing the things that are familiar and comfortable to us. Deviating from our traditional pathways and our neurologically-refined behaviors actually takes work. But the point is that people do it, and so can you.

To be clear, being in the present moment does not necessitate having to withdraw from the people in your life. That would simply be trying to escape the present moment or vainly trying to replace it with another one, and this is no different from the path of addiction. Fundamentally, the *moment* is wherever you happen to be, right now. It is here in the now, and you are already there. You simply have to be receptive to it.

Where the rubber meets the road is when we gather enough clarity in the midst of a chaotic situation to be able to let go of the negative energy that we're currently espousing, and simply turn the mind to what simply *is*.

My child is screaming.

My child is in tears.

My child has not heard anything that I've said.

Two of my kids are in the car, and the other one is still in the backyard.

It's 11pm, and my child is dancing nude in the kitchen.

My kid has lit the curtains on fire.

Granted, these are not moments that a typical person is going to be thrilled to be in. Let's face it, it's not the same thing as being "in the moment" while holidaying on a beach in Mexico. Yet these are the real everyday moments that most of us are actually going to be called to – so it only makes sense that we acknowledge what is actually happening in these moments while also allowing ourselves to *pay attention to the particular beliefs we have about these things*. In this way, mindfulness is not about etherealizing yourself away from the grind, but to instead to find a place of being within that raw, real space of life.

Because no matter what you do, life will find a way to resurface and visit you, time and time again.

Granted, for the parent who is in the process of awakening, it can be all too easy to feel disrupted in the pursuit of a mindful presence. The parent fully realizes the importance of mindfulness, which is why they can end up feeling unexpectedly 'ripped off' when the kids are not cultivating an environment that is conducive to this practice. Yet that's precisely the point I'm making here. If we want our conscious awareness to be anything more than a trendy fad in our lives, then it has to take form *inside* the aggressive heat of the difficult moment itself. It needs to occur within the eye of the storm for it to actually lead towards transformation and growth, otherwise it will always just be something that we're vainly pursuing and chasing, rather than actually owning and mastering.

Bringing it back full circle, then, we can see how such an approach is so valuable for us when it comes to the theme of patience.

Patience is graciously afforded to us by the simple act of acknowledging what is actually happening; not by merely wishing that something different was taking place instead. It is formed and refined by the process of taking the time, in that very moment, to simply just observe what is going on without the added burden of judging it. In practice, this means allowing yourself some time to quietly just watch the scene and also to pay attention to your own inner emotions to it. You are not forcing away your emotions here; you are simply allowing them to be what they are. Notice them, observe them, and by mindfully refraining from acting on them you will find that a pleasant type of inquisitiveness is generated in your mind as a result.

In this way, *curiosity* slowly comes to replace apprehension and panic.

Of course, there are circumstances where some action is required in the moment – especially where kids are concerned. You're obviously not going to just stare at your child while they're actively distressed (that would just make you weird). Likewise, you're not going to just sit there while the curtains are on fire and think to yourself: *'oh look, the curtains are on fire. How am I feeling about that in this moment? Let's watch this for a while.'*

In circumstances where action is needed in the moment itself, the keen artist will move swiftly – not desperately. In these settings, responding to a situation with a quiet, yet natural force is akin to scratching an itch without butchering the skin. It is measured, organic response rather than aggressively plunging in that makes all the difference. Furthermore, consecutive, gradual practice in the art of mindfulness is what develops such an artful skill. When practiced over time, this will surely allow you to respond in more appropriate and natural ways instead of reacting like you've just been shot in the gut.

Consider the theme of thought itself. We're all very familiar with the adage, "think before you act." Yet, I would argue that "thinking" can often get in the way of the most appropriate responses to situations. The fact is, most of us already believe this, albeit unknowingly! For example, why is it that we sometimes find ourselves responding – without thinking – to certain emergency situations that require instant action in the moment? What does it mean when we hear stories of regular, average people who were able to perform inexplicable acts of heroism or who somehow moved in a highly exemplary manner in the face of an environmental or human threat? The fact is that these are moments which call us to simply respond fluidly to a need; not to analyze or dissect it.   In other words, it is to move in a spirit of appropriate response to the recurring swells of life's ocean; releasing ourselves to simply surge upwards and downwards with natural grace at each successive wave. This is our hidden ability, and we all too frequently neglect its power in our personal lives, and in the chaotic moments of our family dynamics.

"There is little chance of misunderstanding where there is quick response to immediate needs." (From the *I Ching*)

What I'm saying is that by practicing being in the genuine now, no matter how chaotic the now might be, you will gradually find yourself moving in tandem with the natural flow of family life and everything that comes along with it. Obviously, you're going to make mistakes. Never forget that. But it's the deliberate commitment to observe and reflect on those mistakes that builds a stronger currency for proper response in the future.

Let the mistake, or the 'failure' as it were, mold you into something stronger and more refined. Allow for your child's behaviors and crises to serve as the greatest informant to your otherwise confused and disoriented persona as a caregiver. These are the true teaching moments that are being gifted to you, despite the discomfort that so often comes along with them. The secret is to simply receive the teaching rather than to fight against it.

This is parenting, in all its glory.

5

Parenting between the Lines

*"I believe that what we become depends on what our fathers teach us
at odd moments, when they aren't trying to teach us."*

\- Umberto Eco

For some unclear reason, early on in the journey of
parenting we somehow come to see our roles as parents
in a rather disproportionate way. We want to foster
their intelligence and guide them in their purest
expression, yet at the same time we are fine with
allowing them to be guided and coached by alternative
forms of media, granting ourselves convenient respite
periods from using our parental insight while their
influential minds are busily soaking up the base humor
of "reality" television, crudely-animated, slang-talking
animals, and the personal musings of an
anthropomorphic sea-sponge. We hope the very best for
them, spending small fortunes on their cultural and
personal development while, paradoxically, we entertain
meals at the table that are loomed over by the stormy
skies of our personal fatigue and the frequent
dissatisfaction of our own contributions to the world (if
we eat together at all, for that matter).

At any rate, we live in a cultural season where parenting
has become an exhausting exercise for the best of us, and

it's all we can do to sustain whatever energy we have left in the face of it all without completely letting go of our values.

I believe most of us wish for our children to be able to appreciate the finer and more richly-defined things in life. Likewise, we want them to be balanced, decent and healthy human beings who are able to serve and lead society into better places; effectively carrying the torch of progress forward into tomorrow's world.

When it comes right down to it, we want to be good parents, but we also want something else.

Good *children*.

Somewhere along the line of our training and programming as parents, we began to view our role most emphatically as dispensers of knowledge and as the mitigating agents of our children's conduct. We unconsciously came to see our job as that of influencer of these small persons; presuming an ownership over their development, yet nevertheless forgetting – all too early in the relationship – that there is just as much need for development to take place in *us*. In due time, we easily forgot that we needed just as much input as they do; that we were in just as much need of an open spirit of exploration and curiosity as they have.

Disproportionate development started to occur, however, when we assumed too much the garb of the *teacher*, per se, rather than that of the student. At certain times, this led to a sense of entitlement on our part. An entitlement over the child's learning journey whereby we began to see ourselves as the proverbial imparter of trivial knowledge to an otherwise open vessel whom we assumed needed to hear and retain all of our parental noise, without any chance for a two-way sharing of ideas or expressions. As such, untempered pride in an overzealous parent can quickly lead to unnecessary fission within a family, resulting in further division between child and parent and ultimately paving the way for a child's need to rebel and to crave distance.

In her book *A Story Lately Told*, the famed actress Angelica Huston opens up about her father, the legendary filmmaker John Huston. A visionary artist who was revered for his directing as well as his screenwriting talents, to his children he was otherwise viewed as a preoccupied, often unstable presence that often needed to be avoided. With sad poignancy, Huston writes about the times in which their family would sit together at the meal table, only to have her father drill his children with random trivia questions; probing for accuracy and concrete knowledge rather than seeking the simple joy of engaging them in conversation.

To John Huston, his children's natural milestones and personal ambitions of self-discovery were sometimes interpreted as threatening gestures; inexplicable deviations from his own preconceived notions about the correct course of growth, which is why they inevitably felt the need to carve out identities for themselves that could be experienced in safer, more remote places away from his decidedly uneven and distorted affections. Huston goes on to describe some very painful periods in her early adult life where, despite abject poverty and the sheer struggle of trying to establish her modeling and acting crafts, she chose not to draw from her father's resources for the simple reason that their bond had been so badly injured that she did not want to have to claim any undue support from him.

Huston implies that her father eventually came to seek a place of reparation in his ties with his children, though it's hard to determine – as the reader – how much of this rapprochement was a conscious one on his part rather than the simple mellowing of disposition that sometimes comes with old age. At any rate, his earlier, more fragmented attempts to act as the pillar in his household bear an uncomfortable resemblance to some of the sordid experiences that many of us, as parents in our own right, may sometimes be guilty of.

Let's face it. Living in trend-setting cultures is something we've always had to deal with as parents, and even the best of us can find it hard to resist the pressures of making our children conform to the expectations that are being created by society. The fact is that we don't want our children to fall behind the rest of their peers, and its human nature to want to see our child excelling in what they do. We don't want them labelled in negative ways, and we get touchy when they exhibit behaviors that seem to take none of this to heart. Eventually, this only breeds further friction between the parent and child until the child either conforms to the norm out of learned fear, or winds up pushing the ejection-seat button from the parents' home at the earliest opportunity in life.

And yet, despite all of this need for space, they do need us to teach them after all.

The guiding principle, however, is not the *content* of the information passed between parent and child, but rather the overall spirit of sharing that is brought to the relationship in the first place. This means that the greater thing that we are bringing into the relationship is the sheer willingness to both deliver as well as receive, insofar as any influencing is concerned. The very fact that we are demonstrating a heart of *vulnerability* and *openness* – an attitude completely void of entitlement in our role – is one of the most potent lessons we can give our children; particularly as we find ourselves in a world where honesty and decency are finding new degrees of currency in lieu of so much of the self-obsessed energy and ego-driven opportunism that has marked our Western culture for so long.

Additionally, it is a fact that we live in an age of manically-delivered information. Unprecedented access to linear forms of knowledge has left us entitled, skeptical and guarded in what we are willing to endorse, and thereby can render us more crippled in our ability to quietly receive opportunities to be genuinely transformed. Essentially, despite all of our apparent progress as a society, it's even harder now to feel more open in our perspectives simply because we see ourselves as so heartily "informed" already. We regard new concepts as suspect, and we sit safely in our personal little cubicles of fixed information and 'proven' methods of seeing the world.

Yet the invitation to be transformed into more expansive and engaged (and more interesting) people is perpetually right in front of us, particularly as parents.

The child transforms you. Your perspectives, your insights, your sense of love and decency are all nurtured and honed by the gradual and incremental effects of how your little boy or girl works on you; counsels you, even. It is through these stunningly rare, few and very messy years of childrearing that we can begin to see glimpses of our former innocence coming to light again – though all too often we blink these insights away in quick deference to the immediacy of the moment; the urgency of the *appointment*. As it happens, these precious drops of insight that are gifted to us daily become routinely sacrificed – vanished altogether even – in the unconscious foray of our everyday lives and our occupations.

Instead of dwelling richly with our loved ones, we dwell instead in a state of manic functionality, calling it 'life with kids' in our desperate quest to get up in the morning - only so that we can go to bed at night only a few moments later. And in those priceless and limited hours that mark our day, we continue to watch helplessly as our children join the ranks of other distracted families, learning more lessons from the collective standards of a dreamless society than from the integrity of their own family (since the family is decidedly too busy and too tired to actively portray their values in a conscious, deliberate form).

In the face of all this exhaustion, compounded by the burdensome norms that exist around us, we leap-frog over the intricate zone of connecting with our child and resort to "teaching" them and advising them on how to be, and how to act. We base our parenting on the formulaic rigors of what is "expected" of our children, rather than what is actually nourishing for them at a deep level. We also send them off to school, daycare and a dizzying blend of extracurricular activities – assuming that all of these things are essential and normal for their healthy steering in life. And while it's true that these things may equip a child with certain tools that serve to unlock the socioeconomic gates of our society's various kingdoms, the underlying fact remains that many of these kingdoms are formed upon standards and ideals that place far more emphasis on the more visible and material qualities of living. As such, a culture of fear and scarcity is formed through the consistent adherence to many of these trends (which are, by their very nature, spiritually unsustainable of their own merit), and we ultimately find ourselves caught in the web of wanting our child to pursue their authentic self while simultaneously wanting them to be accepted by the civilization they happen to find themselves in.

In response to this cultural dilemma, we try to soothe ourselves with the belief that our children are learning how to be 'socialized' among other influencers when the reality is that we are far too distracted to be present with them, and too caught up in life's demands to be otherwise accessible to them (since we are trying to keep up with the socioeconomic demands of the 'kingdom' ourselves). We forgive ourselves for being busy, and we chalk up dysfunctional relations with our kids to the unavoidable conditions of modern reality.

Through all of this messy conditioning, however, we forget that we are the fundamental creators of our own reality.

We observe the cacophony of noise and disorientation going on in the modern world, and it really seems like a normal thing to us. Concepts of human stress, endless schedules, deadlines and financial preoccupation have become a backdrop for our social lives, altogether training and coaching us to *anticipate* feeling scattered and constrained in our adult years. Without a doubt, this feeling of disorientation becomes the 'new normal' that we end up carrying into our exchanges with our children, and through this new sense of normalcy we give license to our unconscious parenting. And yes, while it may indeed "take a village" to raise a single child, who's to say that the 'village' is in the healthiest position to do this, or that they can even begin to appreciate the deeper values and insights that are inherently within you, the parent? Seldom do we ever stop to ask whether the village has its *own* agenda.

The fact is that the community that we happen to find ourselves in, be it geographical, academic, cultural or religious, may not always have our child's particular and unique interests at heart. That may sound harsh or depressing to hear, yet at the end of the day we owe it to ourselves and our families to discern whether we are truly moving in accordance with our own values or whether we're instead giving something away for the benefit of acceptance from the wider group.

The Art of Living

"Wisdom calls aloud outside; She raises her voice in the open squares. She cries out in the chief concourses. At the opening of the gates in the city She speaks her words…" (Proverbs 1:20-21)

We are surrounded by the gift of instruction. Life itself is the greatest teacher that we could ever ask for. Our everyday experiences are ripe with all the wisdom we need, and the natural unfolding of our days brings us into regular contact with streams of higher understanding.

But it doesn't happen automatically. To set ourselves to the soft vibrational frequency of timeless wisdom requires a certain deliberation in our being; a willingness to actually tune ourselves to the rhythm, and have the quiet patience to pay attention to what is being revealed.

Most of us, however, are easily tuned out from aligning ourselves with that instruction, and we unconsciously resign ourselves to a reactionary baseline whereby we live, breathe and eat in direct correlation with the triggers, stimuli, pleasures and pressures that bombard us every single day. In short, we make unconscious choices to live in a state of *function* and consequently spend the better part of our lives acting in accordance with the survival-based hardwiring of our senses. In this way, we learn how to stay afloat and we even learn strategies that help us get the things we want. Sometimes we even figure out how to multiply our returns, and to successfully crush the competition. But then all we ever do is repeat the same silly thing over and over again.

Is it any wonder so many people are depressed and anxious? We're anxious when we feel that we're in scarcity, and we're anxious when we try to maintain *un-scarcity!*

There is a virtual sea of research which discusses the connection between the role of the amygdala (otherwise known as the 'fight, flight or freeze' part of our brains) and our everyday response to the myriad events around us. The layman's explanation is that former, prehistoric impulses to fight off a thieving wolf or to run from a hungry tiger have naturally carried over into our contemporary social environments, leaving us to sometimes overreact in the way that we do, or to interpret something as potentially threatening (such as when somebody cuts in front of us at Starbucks).

The point is that we are so accustomed, from a young age even, to live our lives in a "hit the ground running" sort of fashion, which effectively makes it harder to pay attention to anything else that may be happening on a much quieter level in our environment.

"Stillness reveals the secrets of eternity." (Lao Tzu)

It can be difficult to notice the small daisy flower sprouting up within a tiny crack in the middle of the road, when the road is busily swarming with fast-moving vehicles in the middle of rush hour. And yet, the daisy itself is by far the most profound and vital piece of information within that entire scene. After all, that daisy's appearance represents a vast interchange of geological and biological events and relationships that have essentially been unfolding for an innumerable number of millennia, ultimately resulting in this one striking manifestation, in this brief moment in time. The daisy pays no heed whatsoever to the thundering, mechanical violence that is liable to end its existence at any moment. It simply is, and offers no apologies for being there.

And so it is with our decision to transcend what is happening around us.

When we stop to observe, rather than to react.

That is the revolutionary first step in our awakening.

That is transcendence from what we currently see with the naked eye, in order to perceive the greater essence of what is happening beyond it, and around it. This is something we have every power to initiate, within ourselves, and the wonderful thing is that it is readily available, at a moment's notice.

Take the breath for example. We all know that breathing is a fundamental part of our autonomic nervous system, and that it carries on without our paying any attention to it. Yet the moment we turn our attention to it we suddenly realize how much it is affected by our emotional response to stimuli, whether it be internal or external to ourselves. The glaring look somebody gives us, the unexpected numbers in our bank account statement, the surge of excitement at pleasurable moments - each of these things trigger a profound, physiological reaction. And the reason they trigger such a reaction is because somewhere, deep within the recesses of our brain, we have assigned some kind of meaning to these things. In addition, once we take stock of our breathing and begin directing it in a deliberate fashion, we find that it not only alters our emotional and psychological perspective on things, but it actually influences our physiology as well. In this way, we see the seedlings of our transformation begin to take form.

Raising a child is no different. In fact, raising a child brings with it extremely unique opportunities and blessings for learning and growth for the parent, principally because within the gauntlet of daily rigors associated with the modern parent's role there exists a profound chamber of space and opportunity to become something better and more mature than we otherwise believe is possible. And while it is true that a life without children can certainly provide a copious amount of opportunity to achieve high levels of productivity in the world (be it material, academic or otherwise), it is nevertheless the life of a parent that is especially endowed with a very unique opportunity by which a profound degree of personal transformation can take place. This transformation is not achieved in *spite* of the stressors of child-rearing, nor is it mustered up in frantic, scattered and episodic moments where the parent manages to swipe some quiet "meditation" time for him or herself. On the contrary, true and deep transformation takes form when the parent simply lets go of the burden of expectation, and allows the sheer presence of household reality to be what it naturally is, and to ultimately change the person for the better.

Amazingly, it is this one pivotal process of continual transformation that can have the greatest impact on a child – regardless of how old they are. This is because the child is now released from the suffocating burden of being *expected* to grow in a certain way, and can simply be free to witness and quietly observe the genuine growth of their parent instead. As the parent's focus turns to the art of self-mastery, the angst of coaching their child is taken out of the equation.

Psychologist John Chambers Christopher, writing in a 2018 issue of the *Journal of Theoretical and Philosophical Psychology*, points to an interchangeability in the terms 'mindfulness' and 'releasement.' Drawing primarily from Meister Eckhart's concept of *Gelasenheit*, the basic idea revolves around the sheer acceptance of a thing for what it is, and the absence of either hoping or demanding that it be something else. As Chambers himself explains:

> *"Releasement entails an openness to being, to letting things be. Letting be requires waiting and listening – attentively receiving what is given to us. It is allowing things to show up and be seen in their own terms before we have imposed our agendas, needs, and desires* (Chambers, 2018, p. 62)."

Naturally, he goes on to recount how a pure, willful releasement of these burdens plays a powerful role in inducing a deeper well-being of mind and body. With this new-found wellness of being, then, the practitioner of the art is able to resume not merely the task of parenting – but life itself, for that matter.

It goes without saying that living with kids is not always easy, and sometimes it can even be extremely stressful and emotionally draining. The good news is that if you are finding yourself actually recognizing and identifying some of these things, then you are starting from a very healthy and necessary place. As it is with any success in the art of defense, to know what you are dealing with is to begin the quest of overcoming it.

First of all, sensations of moral deflation and angst usually indicate that we care exponentially about our child and that we want something good for them. The fact that we feel a sense of tearing in our spirit at various junctions of it all demonstrates that, somewhere deep down inside, we know that there is a better way to being with our child; that there is something missing in the overall equation of the family, and that something isn't flowing the way we want it to.

And our maturity is reached once we understand that this is *our* responsibility, and not our child's. The child simply *is*.

Claiming time

It's true that our children can be very forgiving. Somehow they're able to forget the moments when we lose control of ourselves; miraculously finding new ways to reach out to us only moments afterwards. For much of the time, they don't even seem all that fazed by our incessant exhaustion either, and seem perfectly content that we are merely just there in the first place. They can have intense resilience in this regard, something which by their very design bolsters them in their pioneering quest through this fascinating new world that they are discovering. And while this resilience can serve us very well as we make countless mistakes in our parenting efforts, it can nevertheless become all too easy for us to become dependent on this part of their makeup; unconsciously viewing it as a gateway for our continued misdemeanors while consistently neglecting our own development.

This is why the fine craft of parenting is one that involves frequent retreats *within*. It means leaving behind the expectations that your own brain has formulated, and journeying freely into the inner realm of quietness where the truest voice of wisdom is speaking in soft - yet very clear - tones. This is the journey in which you start to become a little more acquainted with your truest self, and by meeting with this self you become increasingly prepared to serve your family in a much higher capacity.

Mothers and fathers are very wise to pursue a simple transcendence above the mundane stresses that come with their vocation. This can be achieved in a variety of ways, though each one involves some degree of meditation and stillness in its approach. And while some readers may challenge me in pointing out that having the time to incorporate these things is not exactly a luxury that we, as parents, typically have – I would counter that assertion with the insistence that we actually *do*.

Plainly speaking, we find ways to make time for the things that are the most important to us, don't we?

In my own experience, raising three boys has given me a massive appreciation for the concept of time itself. As far as linear time is concerned, I had plenty of it when I was in my teens and twenties. Unfortunately, however, I mainly saw fit to use it in ways that didn't exactly bring out the best of my potential. As it turned out, I only began embracing the gift of it once I really saw how powerful a thing it was for one's personal exploration and understanding – though by this time I was no longer single, and was by now deeply immersed in the disorienting vortex of diapers, tantrums, bedtime revolts, stomping feet and disagreeable neighbors living beneath us.

Subsequently, it was through the radical unfolding of these domestic realities that I came to see how my tempestuous relationship with time could either serve to exacerbate my daily stress or, alternatively, it could yet be embraced – perhaps for the first time in my entire life.

If I could put it more simply, it was not until well into my experience as a father that I realized that I had spent shockingly little time in my adult life in taking stock of the *moment*. As best as I can recollect, I don't think I really understood the benefits of true reflection in my years of bachelorhood, and I believe that this tragic lack of perception is one of the biggest factors that led to my endless pursuit of things that really weren't very important in the long run.

By the sheer grace of God, however, I somehow ended up with a wife who – despite having found her when I was hopelessly immature – became my closest and most intimate ally in this entire journey ever since. While I have indeed screwed up many things in my life, I remain humbled and profoundly shocked to this day that my foolishness was not so damaging to the point where I ended up in a disastrous marriage. To the contrary, I consider my marriage to be my greatest asset in life at the moment; the vehicle by which I have been able to experience so many necessary lessons and evolutions in the overall quest of raising a family.

Insofar as time itself is concerned, however, I have had to make determined, conscientious efforts in carving out opportunities for myself for personal meditation, fitness, prayer, and ultimately writing. *Stealing* time would be a good way of describing the process, as it has indeed been like learning a new skill to pull myself away from the daily marathon of life so that I am properly settled in my own space of quietness and stillness. As I already mentioned, in my life this means that 5am is a typical wake-up hour, allowing me a decent period to establish my focus and realign myself with my personal goals.

Additionally, I make it a point to find opportunities while I'm at work, at the store, in the car, and wherever else I happen to be. It's actually remarkable how easy it can be to retreat to the laundry room or to the backyard for the purpose of securing just enough moments to find a place of centering in yourself. It may *seem* hard to secure these moments, but it really comes down to a matter of choice. And while most of these retreats may not look very luxurious or exotic, the point is that they still work. Let's be real here. Trying to make these sessions into some kind of trendy, zen-like artistic expression is just going to stress us out, especially when you've got a kid knocking over block-towers in the next room.

The point is to be able to return to a place of releasing yourself. Simply just releasing, and letting be. Through this releasing, we gradually come closer to a place of trusting in the universe itself. These sessions are to remind us of this fact, and to help us shed the layers of 'expectation' that we quickly adopt over the course of any typical day.

Without a doubt, being able to return to your family after having taken these few moments is by far one of the best things you can do for them, as well as for yourself, chiefly because these little retreats provide such a crucial zone for your most dramatic transformation as a human being. In my opinion, the continued practice of this art is exponentially more valuable than attending any major live-speaking event.

"Sometimes it is best to withdraw, thus preserving your strength."
(From the *I Ching*)

In my own experience, there have been a few times where an intense argument with my wife or with my children has necessitated my complete departure from the house itself. At times like this I have opted to physically walk around the neighborhood while my emotions were fuming and spinning out of control. Plainly speaking, there was just no space in my mind to consider meaningful dialogue during these heated moments, and for me to remain in the house would only have led to an even uglier scene. I share this simply because I feel it's important for you to know that calmness and tranquility do not come easily to me (which is probably why I needed to write a book about it). Whether it's my nature, my past experiences, my own programming or whatever the case may be – my default setting has always been one of high-intensity and apprehensiveness. Traditionally, I was a person who was easily disoriented in mildly stressful situations and who tended to use way too many words in order to compensate for feeling awkward, nervous, or simply just unsure of the situation (which was pretty well most of the time). I remember once overhearing a mutual friend's fiancé – upon meeting me for the first time – remark that I was "the most intense person" he had ever met. I didn't take it as a compliment.

In any event, I have found repeatedly that sometimes all it takes is a brief removal from the hotbed of my home for me to find a bit of clarity. Doing something – *anything* – to temporarily deflect your energy away from the conflict is akin to shutting off the pressure valve in your system. If, at the very least, you give yourself some space to let the emotion drain itself off naturally, and allow the cortisol to run its course without adding to it, you may find that your perspective on the situation begins to shift very quickly.

This is because of the simple fact that tension already starts to become dissolved once a clean space is permitted. The important thing to bear in mind, however, is that this shift needs to coincide with a perspective of *humility*. Humility is essential for your success in returning to the domestic milieu of your household and to be able to assume a more cooperative disposition. Make no mistake. Your family needs the *humbled* you; not the psychologically-abusive bastard that comes all too easily for some of us.

And yes, I know there are many who will question whether it's truly our partner or our disobedient child who is the more culpable party in any given conflict, but the thing to remember is that we – as parents – are not in the business of *proving* something to our loved ones. If it's all about proving a point, then we have no business being with these particular loved ones in this moment, regardless of how much we may love them. As I emphasize elsewhere in this book, 'love' is not the question here. Our heart may be filled with love while our entire spirit is completely misaligned with what our family actually needs. If we really want to get down to the true business of domestic management, the singular principle here is *personal responsibility*.

Additionally, if we are talking about you and your partner having a major disagreement, common sense alone dictates that you will get absolutely nowhere by coming back with a renewed zeal in your original argument. To be sure, the whole point of this is not to 'master' your partner; it is to master the self. Your partner, if they truly are in the wrong, will only ever come to a healthier perspective if you – in turn – allow *them* the space to recalibrate and retreat into where they need to go to find it.

To clarify, the work is always on your *own* self. Do this work first, and the others will have the finest light to emulate and follow; in their own time.

The other aspect of retreating into personal inner space is that you are essentially telling your spouse and your child (and yourself for that matter) that you are highly invested in them, and that you regard them as the immediate benefactors of your very best self. For this reason, you are committed to the excursion into your own space in order to find rehabilitation from your own self-inflicted injuries, and to essentially find a reconnection with your soul. Sometimes it takes all but a few brief moments for disorientation to wash away from you and for clarity to flood your mind, giving you the strength and the humility you need to return to your loved ones and take your honorable place.

The more you practice this, the more fluid it becomes over time. Your child will grow from this.

Seek honor. Seek transparency.

You will never need a hiding place.

6

At Peace with Transition

"Analysis does not transform consciousness."

– Jiddu Krishnamurti

It would appear that parents, in many ways, are brought into this world with very little to guide them in their new employment as caregivers. This is quite an astonishing thing when you stop to think about it, especially given the fact that the job they're about to take on has arguably been one of the most important occupations since the dawn of the human race. Our children come to us when we presumably don't have the answers, the life experience, or even the sense of readiness to begin working with them. They just come. And while we live in a society that has seemingly become quite skilled at 'planning' birth, we are nevertheless thrown into a vast maelstrom of disorienting debates and opinions about what to do once our baby is actually born.

So what *can* we expect when we're expecting? Well, no matter what schematic you might confabulate in your mind, get ready to jettison it out the window very quickly.

Better yet, just hand it to your newborn. He'll toss it *for* you.

It's not that I'm downplaying advice or personal anecdotes that have universal application, or even books on the subject (I've asked you to read *this* after all). I'm simply making the point that, no matter how well prepared we might be, we have absolutely no idea what this unique and wonderful little creature is going to bring to us, nor can we fathom the degree of character formation we will be invited to engage in for ourselves. I marvel even today on how radically different my own three boys are from each other, and the only lesson I have on adjusting one's parenting is by simply *living* the process and *receiving* it as it plays out every day.

Living and receiving.

Life itself provides the answers, as long as we're able to listen. It really comes down to that one essential thing. If I can summarize what fatherhood has done for me as a human being, it's that it has been a monumental catalyst for the deepest personal change.

Over these past few years of fathering, I've come to really appreciate the way in which the phenomenon of human influence seems to go both ways when it comes to parent and child. I think I really had a hard time facing this reality in the early segment of my oldest child's development, and probably to some extent still today, if I'm being completely honest.

My harsh resistance to the concept that my child could ever possibly influence my own decision-making was likely forged from my earlier years of growing up in a fairly rigid, somewhat fundamentalist religious community. Where I came from, a child was expected to be the silent recipient; the blank canvas upon which the acrylics of the eldership should have full rights to portray their values and beliefs – no matter how unhealthy or devoid of social reality they may actually be. For me, resisting the tutorage of my elders and guardians was akin to rebellion – and it was generally discouraged to attempt to question the ideas of those who were older than me. I'm sure that I eventually learned "acceptable" ways of challenging the opinions and expectations of those within my religious group, yet I – like many others - was careful not to stray too far from the central tenets and understandings that bound our community together. So, to some extent, you could walk your questions forward, but you better not walk too far.

Asher (my eldest) came into my life when I was still very much entrenched in the belief that influencing was a one-way street between parent and child. Suffice it to say that my early years of fatherhood were like a major cleanse diet in which all of my earlier programming had to be gradually flushed out in order for me to start finding a genuine sense of peace in what I was doing as a parent. Inevitably, this process led to some fairly distressing relations between my son and I, with more intellect-clashing than I would care to admit.

Perhaps one of the most important things I learned through this process, however, was the fact that a divergence in perspectives and personas is healthy and even necessary for human expansion. I was once so distracted by the glaring fact that my son was a different type of person than I was, and it really took me a long

91

time to stop seeing this difference as a threat to my capacity as a father. Furthermore, I had to eventually recognize the necessity for him to not only express his individuality, but to also advocate for it passionately when my own stupidity was trying to shut it down.

Truth waits patiently

Somehow, when we open ourselves up to it, truth finds a way to penetrate into our hearts and turn our attention in the right direction. If we're truly receptive to this, then our kids will serve as an amazing catalyst for this phenomenon. Through all their naked perceptions of the world around them, a child cannot help but observe and reflect with a type of wonder that many of us have long since lost – and perhaps even unwittingly tried to forget.

From a child's perspective, however, not only are certain things possible, they actually *should* be done! This is because children do not view possibility through the same restrictive and protective lenses we do. Furthermore, a child is often very quick to point out our own inconsistencies and glaring omissions when we stray from the mark of our own ambitions and goals - something we are careful to gloss over in our vain efforts to protect ourselves. This is just another example of how lasting transcendence from the shallow self can sometimes only occur when pressed by the scorching heat of truth, in all its un-tempered brutality. Sometimes a child's brutal honesty is all the invitation we need in order to authentically grow. So through our attendance to truth, despite how discomforting it may be at times, we thereby give the best moral example to our child that we can. If we can give our child nothing else in life, then we should at least give them this example of adherence.

In effect, what we should ultimately be giving them is the sacred example of being honest with our own selves – especially considering that they are growing up in a world where they will be exposed to plenty examples of blatant lack of self-mastery, not to mention the countless opportunities for self-fakery.

Thinking about this kind of thing demonstrates how being a parent to a child is simply one of the most mind-bending forms of education that one will ever experience in their lifetime. Assuming, of course, that one is prepared to shed the belief that the relationship should be a one-way street of transferring wisdom and knowledge, or of rigidly viewing the roles of parent and child as that of 'teacher' and 'student,' for that matter.

Truly, it is *soul* education at one of the highest levels, in my opinion, so long as we have the wherewithal in our human spirit to allow it to be so. Being a parent brings with it the opportunity for an endless array of character shifts; not to mention the benefit of having one's perspective on the world enhanced in unexpected ways. This is not to say that the process is always peaceful or euphoric, however. On the contrary, the very fact that this is often *not* the way it plays out is a testament to how true growth is achieved in the face of challenge, sheer difficulty, and sometimes blatant disorientation.

Obviously, there are parents out there who resist this education quite vehemently. I remember sitting in Starbucks one day overhearing the impassioned discussion between a group of forty-somethings. The subject was on children, and I remember listening to one particular woman bemoan the fact that "children suck the life right out of you." She went on to reflect that there is so much that she could have accomplished in her life if it were not for having children!

Granted, I have no idea what kind of day this woman was having, or what kind of adversities she has had to deal with in her own life, but her comment was jarring enough to remind me that hers is not very uncommon in today's world of the modern parent. She was simply saying what many others are merely thinking, and it's a testament to how fragmented we have generally become in our ability to enjoy the holistic nature of actually *being* a family. I distinctly remember a colleague of mine several years ago who flatly stated: "there's no part of parenting that I enjoyed." I would suggest that this is one of the reasons why we've built such a strong culture around farming our kids out to various institutions, programs and sporting events. It's why we shuttle them to daycare, set up playdates, occupy them with screens and feed them with fast-food in order to keep them contained, sedated, and routed consistently enough in their pens so that they intrude on our precious adult spaces as infrequently as possible.

I'll admit there are times when I'll find myself sliding down a slippery slope of complaining about being incessantly preoccupied with the demands of parenting, yet I'll be the first person to say that it is more often than not the subtle example of my own child that serves to jumpstart my ego back into a better, healthier alignment. Counterintuitive as it may sound, the best solvent for a de-programmed parent is the honesty of simply just being with your child and letting go of everything else that's going on around you. As Fyodor Dostoyevsky once said, "*the soul is healed by being with children.*"

94

I have come to discover that my children teach me far more than I ever thought possible, and that they truly do save my life on a daily basis. Essentially, it is through their unique and unwitting counsel to *me*, through countless casual sermons and innocent observances, that I find a lusty renewal in my personal quest for mastery.

And sometimes their counsel is not so subtle, I might add. Let's face it. Children have crises, and they throw accusations at us that sting and leave a mark. Yet the gift in all of this is that, through even the most disturbed-seeming displays of behavior that we see in our child, we are being redirected back to a place of alignment within our own selves. Often, the "bad" behavior in our child is a stunning opportunity to view the mirrored angst and tension that exists in our own selves. The difference is that we've learned how to hide it from our own perception over the years while our child, on the other hand, is simply living it out in full expression, without any apologies whatsoever. Within this space of expression the child is actually helping us to re-examine our own angst and disturbance, and to simply be honest about it for the sake of healthfully moving beyond it.

Bringing it down to the level of the practical, this dramatic interplay between parent and child is such that it can lead the parent ever more closely towards self-awareness. Additionally, it can bring the parent to an eventual place of pure clarity whereby they are better equipped to respond to their innermost needs.

So, yes, even tantrums can be helpful for us! The essential principle, however, is to remember to keep asking ourselves the question of what this tantrum is really teaching us about our own selves. In other words, what is being mirrored back to me in this loud, visceral masterpiece of human emotion coming from my child? Finally, what example will I be manifesting out into the universe (and my child for that matter) by my choice to pay attention to it, or to instead ignore it?

And therein lies the 'rub,' as they say.

Simply put, there is something very profound and beautifully silent that is happening within the proverbial kitchen of our daily family experiences. Somehow, amidst the chaotic noise of meal preparations and the brain cell-depleting experience of getting kids out the door, there's a remarkable dance that's taking place between the occupants of the home. It's at the root of this very dance that we are blessed with the opportunity to move beyond the confines of the struggle itself, and to simply allow ourselves to be guided into a more poignant moment of family development. The challenge, however, is to hold onto these moments and regard them for the treasures they really are while not letting the cyclical tides of stress become the focus of one's intellect.

'Guided' is the key word here, since it discards the context of anything forced or pressured into being. After all, we can apply mental and physical labor in getting our children packed up and out the door but, more often than not, the moments that follow are not very satisfying for any of us. In my own experience, it's times like these where finally getting my boys buckled in the car has left me with a feeling not unlike the experience of a personal trauma, or a psychological breakdown, even. Sometimes it really does feel like I'm about to have a stroke, and the task of coming down from that degree of stress becomes a detoxification process in and of itself. And, oh, what fun *that* is for my family!

Resistance is futile

Those moments where the situation seems to demand some kind of struggle are *precisely* the moments that are pregnant with the opportunity for our awakening. It begins with reminding ourselves that the perception of a struggle, to begin with, is merely a distraction. Alas, even these tension-filled moments carry the prospect of wisdom for us.

We begin by just asking ourselves about how the struggle has come about in the first place? In what ways did it materialize?

For one thing, wisdom begins by simply posing the honest question of whether our child is genuinely being oppositional in this situation. Is their expectation of the situation truly unreasonable? Maybe it is. But that's beside the point. My wife, more often than I care to admit, has had to remind me on multiple occasions that my children are precisely that: *children*. While it may sound kind of pathetic, this very basic and most obvious point that she has felt the need to emphasize for my personal benefit always seems to catch me off guard. In the moment of hearing it, it's like I'm just realizing it for the first time.

"Brett...he's a child. That's why he's doing that."

And there it is. A revelation. A new dawn of understanding which, despite its primal simplicity, seems to hit me like two pints of Ayahuasca every time I hear it.

You mean I can't reason with him like I can with my mechanic? Why on earth *not*?

The point is that no matter what we may personally feel about their resistance, or their reason for resisting in the first place, the fact remains that whatever they are bringing to the situation is simply a mosaic, a compilation, of a myriad thoughts, expectations and desires. They won't understand much of these things, necessarily, but they are there nonetheless and our child is dealing with them in the only way they can process for now. Depending on the child, the experience of transition can be an uprooting sensation; a departure from something treasured, familiar or safe. And that's just where they're at. End of story.

The pristine wisdom of a child is such that they see absolutely no need whatsoever to change what they're doing, so long as they feel happy and alive doing it. There's no timeline, as far as they're concerned. For the younger ones in particular, there are no schedules, no deadlines, and no thoughts about having to give time for the possibility of extra traffic on the road. As Kahlil Gibran captured it so well, *"your children are not your children. They are the sons and daughters of Life's longing for itself. You may house their bodies but not their souls, for their souls dwell in the house of tomorrow, which you cannot visit, not even in your dreams."* In other words, the timeless plight of a parent is to be able to discern the subtle ways in which an adult's world has come to diverge so dramatically from that of the child's, and to therefore find a way to honor that sacred place where the child still is. Because, in many senses, *that* is the place we are all trying to return to, after all. The zone of pure living; the innocence of simply being in life.

The challenge for myself, personally, is not to automatically interpret this behavior as a sign of blatant disregard or disrespect. It simply just is. It doesn't matter if we try explaining to the child that the transition is towards something that they would enjoy or that they were previously looking forward to. Their resistance is not about that. It's a response to a change in the *flow* of what they're currently doing, and what we're seeing in them is essentially the reflection of our *own* response to such a shift as adults.

First of all, we need to accept the fact that a child needs *flow* in their life. A kid needs to have their *zone*. A child should have many opportunities to freely find their zone and get carried away in the sheer peaceful energy of it. We need to appreciate that these periods in our child's day are therapeutic for them in terms of coming down from all the stressful energy that we, as adults, bring into their lives. It also goes without saying that these states of flow are developmentally crucial as well.

And I'm not talking about when a child plays a video game, either, or when they're being entertained by some kind of electronic media or through a screen. This is not flow; it's merely distraction. Moreover, it only makes it harder for a child to actually *find* flow in the first place. But when a child is permitted the liberty and the respect to live without having to rely on such vices, they tend to find many other things to occupy themselves with.

With this in mind, flow can look like many things to various children.

Reading. Coloring. Drawing. Cutting. Repeating certain motions. Singing and humming. Digging in the dirt. Tying knots. Watching something natural taking place in their environment. Walking in circles while mumbling some inaudible story or action sequence which only they are aware of.

Through any of these things (and countless more) a child learns their way. We can't begin to interpret what is really going on in these moments, but it's enough for us to know that the uninterrupted flow of these experiences is vitally restorative and incremental to our child's overall growth and wellbeing.

One of the most amazing books I've ever read was *Son Rise*, by Barry Neil Kaufman. The book is essentially a personalized record of Kaufman's odyssey in steering his toddler out of the vortex of Autism Spectrum Disorder, albeit in what many would consider to be very controversial means.

One of the classical features of autistic behavior is the use of patterned movements (stereotypy) as a way of relating with and managing their external environment. Where many would try to discourage, modify or "schedule" appropriate times for such behavior, Kaufman and his wife basically adopted a program where they not only embraced the stereotypy in their son, but actually went to the unusual lengths of mimicking it themselves in his presence. In essence, their son initiated the cues in accordance with his own temperament, and his parents followed suite in the moment. As you can imagine, this required a significant overhaul in their daily rhythm – not to mention their professional lives – yet the result, as has been documented, is that their son eventually recovered from the syndrome and went on to become a highly-regarded spokesperson for autism recovery.

One of the many take-aways from the Kaufman family's experience should be the awareness that while autistic obsession-play is really an exacerbation of natural, expressive play, a parents' willingness to respect and promote the "zone" of that space is so important for any child. As it was with Barry Kaufman, whatever resistance his child was having to wrestle with in his own life was helped through a gradual, safe space of trust, patience and the sheer permission to simply just be. The point of application for us is that we need to respect and give plenty of space for a child to express. These are the key moments where they find a freedom to 'heal themselves,' as it were, from the unconscious shrapnel of our own mistakes and recoveries as parents.

In essence, let's not find it too threatening when our child resists the call to make a transition. As harrowing as the scene might be sometimes, the best thing to do is move forward and be patient with their resistance. And while we may not actually feel very patient in the moment, the secret is to carry out the job in an *expression* that is both firm and quiet. Do not get caught up in a flurry of dialogue and negotiations, or idle threats. We only find ourselves further adrift when we do this.

And always use fewer words.

But let's just look at this whole thing from a wider lens for a moment. Change is not something we are necessarily in love with in our modern culture. As adults, we sometimes find ourselves facing life's detours and shifts with a certain degree of hesitancy and forbearance. Despite our intelligence and our rational expectation of change in our lives, this does not mean that we're always greeting life's various interruptions and re-adjustments with open arms and a beaming face. It disrupts us. It stresses us. We often feel disoriented with how things pan out, and we quickly allow them to take on mythically-proportionate meanings to the point where we can become a little crazy at times.

Consequently, how do we deal with stress today? Honestly, what do we physically do with ourselves in order to feel relieved from the cacophony of shifts, interruptions, hostilities, late arrivals and early departures that we deal with on a daily basis? Do we not seek some kind of opiate that we know will help to take away some of the accumulated discomfort that we've been shouldering? Furthermore, whatever 'pill' we're taking to distract us (whether in liquid, solid or digital form), does it ultimately serve to help us bridge the waters of change, or does it instead produce an artificial 'change' of its own accord?

Maybe it only distracts us even further; to the point where we become even less equipped to roll with the next series of changes that come our way. And around and around we go.

We come into this world, and very quickly we start to live these distracted lives – all too often as a result of our own parents' fears and misconceptions about the world.

We become distracted from our true selves, from our true passions and our authentic hungers, and we default to one of two extremes: either we seek to be in sync with other people's values and norms, or we spend our life fighting a constant battle with the whole world because of how it's made us feel. Drawing from a more extreme example, I've had enough conversations with people in recovery from drug addiction to know that sometimes these distortions are thrust upon us to such a degree as a child that it proves to be an even harder task of pioneering some way out of it as a result of that experience. But regardless of any of these experiences, I really do believe that if you were to somehow go back and talk to that earliest childhood version of yourself you would find a miraculous and wonderful description of the real person you're supposed to be. That includes your deepest passions and your insatiable curiosity about the things that interest you.

The point is that none of us have any control over the things that have already happened to us. They've happened. They're done. It's already a part of your experience and there is no amount of groaning about it that will ever change that. So just embrace the fact that it has informed you in some way – regardless of the inconvenience and pain that it may have entailed along the way – and allow yourself to experience the critical *now* of where you are. Because it is in the very now of life where you will find the purest opportunity for changing your patterns, your views and your behaviors into something that is truly better. Truth and wisdom will speak to you in this place, and they will provide you with the direction you need for healthy change.

Yesterday can only ever simply educate you. Today, however, is where *everything* takes a new turn.

Without a doubt, no meaningful growth in a human being can take place when there is a determined aversion to change.

Embrace change

"Life is a series of natural and spontaneous changes. Don't resist them; that only creates sorrow. Let reality be reality. Let things flow naturally forward in whatever way they like." - Lao Tzu

Change is no different from taking a breath. Without thinking about it, we receive oxygen into our lungs and then into our blood stream, thereby feeding our corporeal self with elements of the physical universe that are constantly in a state of subatomic flux.

Flux and change are things that are so natural and intrinsically wired into the universe. We can't ignore it. Consider the fact that every part of your body, on the molecular level, is constantly shifting. Tissue is dying off, only to be replaced by new matter. Cells are always being generated; covering every ounce of your frame with newer and newer entities. Blood cells are forever bringing microscopic packets of oxygenated information all throughout your body. Literally speaking, the body that you are sitting in right now is completely different from the one you were living in a year ago. Putting it bluntly, our body is in a consistent state of being broken down and rebuilt, over and over again. It's designed to do this. We are constantly transforming, but we often don't think about this because we have a hard time seeing it with the naked eye.

We break down, and we rebuild. That's just what we do. There is death on many necessary levels, and there is also resurrection.

Many sages have written about the principle of taking ownership of the breakdown process as it manifests in our personal lives. The idea is that we each go through a death state, only to then be rebirthed afterwards. Something has come to an end, and has served to give birth to something new. The truth is that we go through life experiencing many deaths, really, and with those deaths comes the promise of many new resurrections. We cycle through these things on a perpetual basis, yet the *quality* of renewal that we experience depends largely on us and how we choose to roll with those cycles and seasons.

The essential question is whether our subconscious interprets those changes as threats; things to be resisted as we struggle to hang on to whatever is familiar and predictable. Alternatively, has our mind come to embrace this principle, recognizing it for the cleansing, healing phenomenon that it truly is?

Victor Hugo wrote that *"nations, like stars, are entitled to eclipse. All is well, provided the light returns and the eclipse does not become endless night. Dawn and resurrection are synonymous. The reappearance of the light is the same as the survival of the soul."*

Think about this from the perspective of our own growth and maturity as human beings. Every day we are presented with significant events and circumstances that have a powerful potential to teach us new things and to carry us into alternate states of being. If there's anything utterly foreign and alien to our natural agency as human beings, it's the concept of lying dormant or having a total absence from change whatsoever. Whether we like it or not, you and I are moving somewhere in life, and we will always be moving. The amazing thing is that you actually get to *invest in the ride* if you want to. You get to be real about what you really want in life, and where you want to go. That's up to you completely.

Bringing it back to the kitchen, then, we can ask what it is that our children see when they look at us. Do they see a figure who embraces transition and change with a sense of peace and excitement? Or are they simply mimicking a parent who has instead practiced a chronic pattern of stress-response to the demands of life? Or perhaps, as many of us can attest, a subtle form of neurosis? In other words, through our own exhibitions and patterns, have we taught our children to roll with the organic shifting of time and seasons, or have we instead painted the object of transition as a jarring consequence of life? Something that is not very enjoyable or meaningful? Something threatening, perhaps.

Sure, we try convincing them of the plain logic of moving forward, but we forget that they're taking a far greater cue from our actions than from the abrupt mess of words falling clumsily from our mouth.

But, critically speaking, the question must always be redirected back to us as parents. What is it that *we* are resisting here? What is it about our personal lives that our child somehow, seemingly by miraculous depth of perception, has rooted out and is now trying to process themselves?

Conversely, what have *we* given our child to wrestle with?

The good news is that we don't actually have to go back and start mechanically dissecting every part of our psychology over this. We just need to take stock of the moment, cherish the opportunity presented to us, and move forward with it. As I've said it before, child-rearing really begins with the parenting of our own selves. By taking sincere stock of this first principle, we will instantly begin to be a better parent to our child. And the simple reason for this is because true connection never happens by proxy. That is, two agencies cannot meet with each other authentically when they are engaging purely on the level of formalities and bureaucratic policy. When a parent's engagement with their child is carried out purely within the constraints of familial expectations and household norms of conduct, the child is not likely to want to ingest it at a great level. They may hear what's being said, and they may even act in accordance with it, but we're not going to actually *reach* them in a way that makes them feel heard and acknowledged.

This is why it's the *hearing* of a child that is far more important than getting caught up in the temporary infractions of one's code of conduct. While the latter theme should not go completely ignored, it's the focus on the former principle that will actually help pave the way for greater attachment down the road.

Researchers Campbell, Leonard and Thoburn, in a 2017 issue of the journal *Couple and Family Psychology*, demonstrated how simple attributes such as attunement and responsiveness in a parent are strongly linked to their personal level of mindfulness as a caregiver. The researchers ultimately argue that a successful ability to be attuned to one's child, in addition to being able to respond appropriately to them is most likely achieved through a diminished degree of parental stress. In addition, parental stress is significantly diminished through the practice of *mindfulness*. In other words, as simple as it sounds, tuning in to your child works better when you're practicing mindfulness rather than mind*less*ness!

Let me clarify that our children really do depend on us for guidance. After all, I'm not trying to claim the complete other end of the influence spectrum (that we have somehow now become the student of the child, exclusively). At the end of the day, the cosmic arrangement is such that a vulnerable, mortal creature is gifted into our hands and we are left to orient him or her into the vast tapestry of creation. Whatever silent, ancient wisdom is bestowed on them prior to birth is such that we – as developed elders – have a responsibility to discern, recognize, and ultimately help nourish. Furthermore, the way in which we extract the oil from this metaphorical olive becomes, retroactively, the very means by which our children learn to draw new wisdom through their home environment. In essence, they are bringing something into this world that they are not yet able to articulate. This implies that part of our job as a parent, then, is to help them harvest and reap that ancient wisdom so that it can successfully take root and grow throughout that child's life.

Again, this is not a complicated process. The child will actually do most of the work themselves, yet the critical thing is that they need a nurturing space in their life to do it. As awakened parents, our finest hour is when we are able to provide that very space for them to make the discovery for themselves.

Practically speaking, invite yourself to start practicing the art of stalling your response to your child's resistance. Setting aside the pressure of becoming any kind of guru, yogi, or Super Nanny, just start holding back from your typical style of reacting to the opposition. I mean, does it really make sense to meet opposition with opposition? Will that really resonate with their synthesizing mind? What's the worst that will happen by holding off from standing your ground? You might be a little bit off schedule? The worst case scenario is that you just may end up teaching your child that life shouldn't be dictated by programming and rigid scheduling.

And let's get real about anger here. I'm not going to pretend that I don't ever get angry at my kids. But I know for a fact that there is not one single occasion that I can recall where getting angry at my child made me feel healthy or wiser as a result. In fact, I can honestly say that every time where I resorted to yelling or impatient behavior, I ended up feeling noticeably off-balance and out-of-sync with my own intrapersonal ecosystem. Furthermore, I ended up feeling the furthest away from the figure of a "father" than I ever care to experience.

Yet this is a practice. A rhythm that we grow into over time as we gradually put it into play. But we do need to put it into practice, otherwise the traditional cycle we have already built will only just keep repeating itself. Healthy change is only made real when we move on from the intellectual appreciation of a thing, and actually start living by it instead.

So stall your response; especially when you feel the tension and the heat rising up in your bodily system, and when you begin to feel the impatience coming on. Don't worry about trying to dismiss the impatience either. Get real with it, own it, and acknowledge it – but don't let it have the dominion over you. We will live very stunted lives indeed if we feign our natural emotions. These will heal over time as we begin to move through the processes of observing ourselves and making mindful adjustments accordingly.

Start now. Start slowly, and let yourself stumble through. The result is that you will start to experience a greater level of patience for your child, and even a finer love for yourself in the process.

Awakening is a choice

Making the shift from a reactive form of parenting to a more conscious and centered one has not been the easiest thing for me. I think it's true that even the most dysfunctional parents will often have a strong, visceral love for their child, but unfortunately some are unable to translate this love into an energy that is appropriate to their child's needs. In this sense, it is simply not enough to just "love" your child and expect that emotional feeling to somehow decode itself into appropriate and healthy caregiving.

In my own experiences, there have been many occasions where I found myself feeling such overwhelming love and affection to my children during moments where I was physically distant from them, only to startle myself by unexpectedly behaving in some rather negative ways toward them within minutes of being in their presence again, long after I've already spent the better parts of my energy and resources in another vocation that day. In almost every single case where I reacted harshly or impatiently towards my children, I can honestly say that I was acting from a place of very low consciousness, and without any prior effort on my part to simply just center myself without getting caught up in either the past or the future.

This is why the parent who is deeply invested in harvesting their relationship with their child understands that the natural connection which initially exists between child and parent is not always a self-sustaining one, necessarily. Similar to a marriage, it requires a mindful fostering as well as a daily adaptation to the individual needs and dispositions that are unique to the other person. It is a spirit of sincere appreciation and acceptance for who that individual is, in the absence of any preconception of who we think they *should* be. Furthermore, it is an attitude of giving; without any expectation of what the child may give back to us.

Naturally, this may fly in the face of so much of the 'wisdom' passed down to us from our own parents. Any talk of "adapting" to a child's disposition can sound like wholesale heresy to members of the previous

111

generation, and can seem like we're just letting our kids wear the pants *for* us. And to be sure, some due credit certainly needs to go to our hardworking elder generations – particularly since it was largely their concept of personal work ethic and sense of moral values that helped steer the course of prosperity for many of our communities today. So many of our parents grew up in social contexts that were highly influenced by the realities of war and economic instability, which often meant that their childhoods were cultivated with an appreciation for just how easily community and security can be shaken by larger factors.

At the same token, however, it needs to be remembered that the values and social responses of one era do not necessarily translate into appropriate methods and approaches to conflict in another. To a certain extent, there has been a substantial amount of collective, psychological baggage that has been carried over from the last several decades – and one of the most graphic contexts in which this baggage has been unpacked is within the most intimate domain of the family system.

In a sense, you could say that we were, quite often, the direct recipients of our parents' impassioned need to embrace security (and it goes without saying that this need did not start with our parents, but rather with *their* parents) and that we ourselves are now left to sort out whether those historical pressures that *they* lived in are even still applicable and relevant to us today. To that effect, how relevant were they even then? More appropriately, are they relevant to the children we are currently trying to bring up?

And I'm not downplaying the seriousness of what our grandparents lived through either, nor am I dismissing the magnitude of some of the events which took place over the course of the 20th Century. By sheer necessity, a social response was only inevitable in the face of some of those crises, and it was through many of the standards adopted on the family front that helped pioneer some very good and necessary directions forward. But as it is with any journey into new frontiers (such as it is with the spirit of progress in general), true exploration and discovery cannot be achieved when the current group insists on using the systems and methods that were identical to previous cohort groups. This does not lead to new directions, and it will only be harder to uncover new information about our potential as human beings. Essentially, to continue piggy-backing on the value systems of our most recent progenitors is to merely stunt our own progressive journey into the future.

In my opinion, there is simply far too much at stake in terms of our personal conscious awakening for us to be caught up in the same degree of economic and political preoccupation that has impacted our world for as long as it has. Lessons were learned, and discoveries were made. But now it is time for us to have the maturity of mind and spirit to continue taking steps in *our* generation, and to trust that life really does unfold in very positive ways when we release ourselves to the abundantly-maternal whim of the universe. I am a firm believer that the universe is amazingly *in favor* of humanity and that, ironically, sometimes the sheer friction of life is intended to remind us of this.

Sometimes we are the only ones in our circle or community who are receptive enough to realize this, though it doesn't make it any easier, necessarily. With that in mind, the child who has been blessed with the sheer space to simply *be* is the child who has ample room to grow and feel loved. This isn't the same thing as neglecting, or even passively parenting, mind you. As with anything, it is carried out with an approach towards balance. You give the child freedom to express naturally and openly, yet you are mindfully present with them and accessible to them when they need you.

Through this interplay of loving, accepting and *minding*, you facilitate a free space for your child to explore appropriate responses to their environment. And yes, somewhere within this space you are required to step in and mediate, redirect and even discipline at times – but that is yours to work out, and not for me to give counsel. I have simply offered these written words with the appreciation that you are conscious enough to navigate the specific needs and tastes of *your* own personal family, and I am simply here to assure you to keep doing what you are doing. If you have bothered to read this far, it suggests to me that you are serious about the role of awakening in every facet of life to begin with, and that alone implies that you are already in a position of receiving wisdom.

Essentially, it is the very vocation of *being* a parent that provides the spark for initiating new discoveries; new ways of exploring our world and, ultimately, our humanity. Raising a child, by its very rugged nature and messy sophistication, compels us to reach deep within ourselves for the better and truer self – while simultaneously challenging us to observe and transcend our egoic way of responding to our own environment and stressors in the process.

Let me conclude this chapter by pointing out that we are tasked with fostering the furtherance of nurturance in the world as a whole. The best way of describing the spirit of this employment, perhaps, is by likening it to a gardener. One cannot force or insist the blossoming of any flower. It merely blossoms of its own accord – yet cannot grow whatsoever if there is no proper soil or habitation for it to prosper. It will otherwise forever remain only *potential*. And such is parenting.

7

The Fakery of an Ordered Home

*"And this mess is so big and so deep and so tall, we cannot pick it up.
There is no way at all!"*

– The Cat in the Hat

I've always been a stickler for tidiness and order, ever since my early youth. I pick things up off the floor the moment it appears, and will usually wipe off unclean surfaces whenever I come across them. I'm quick to shuffle a pile of papers into their proper order, sorting through them at a rapid-fire pace so as to minimize any unnecessary clutter, and I usually straighten chairs and coffee tables that are out of place. I tend to ensure that bedding surfaces are unwrinkled and neatly tucked in, and I'm one of those guys who will *always* readjust a picture on the wall the moment it appears misaligned.

There's an electrical outlet hidden behind one of the bedside tables in our bedroom at home. Just the other day I questioned my wife on why she had decided to plug our portable air purifier into that particular outlet, thereby leaving our bedside table at a slightly crooked angle from the wall. "You know," I began, "there's a perfectly good outlet on the other side of the room."

The truth is that this little problem had actually been bothering me for a couple of weeks before I finally cracked and said something about it, in a hopeful aim of quelling my mounting anxiety over the issue. Up until that point I had simply just unplugged the purifier every time I walked into the room and plugged it into the other outlet that wasn't being used. The problem, however, was that my wife wasn't getting the hint. *Crap*.

I couldn't help but notice yesterday when I walked into our bedroom and was instantly struck by the fact that not only was the air purifier plugged in, yet again, to my wife's favored outlet, but that the bedside table was mysteriously straightened against the wall. Upon closer examination of this mystifying alignment, I discovered that she had moved the bedside table about two inches closer to the bed, thereby giving the electrical outlet just enough exposure to be used without upsetting our furniture arrangements.

This was a comforting moment for me.

Generally speaking, I will often leave a room about 43% more organized than it was before I walked into it. I remember once as a teenager when a friend of mine once coaxed another friend to turn one of the wall paintings in my parents' house at a slight angle while I was in another room. True to form, I apparently did not miss a beat in tweaking the altered painting as I walked by, or so I was later told.

For me, this is simply my baseline way of managing my surroundings. It's automatic for me. I like things clean, ordered, and with as minimal clutter as possible. I believe in the value of having a meaningful degree of space around various household objects - partly so as to better appreciate their form and purpose – and I don't like too much artificial lighting to be cast upon my environment. Natural light is perfectly fine, and I dislike having too many lights turned on when there is ample sunlight coming in through the windows.

I might be kind of an oddity in this regard, and I also appreciate the borderline obsessive-compulsive impression this might portray to some. Yet it's simply how I've always remembered being. It's just my natural way of orchestrating my personal milieu, and for this reason I don't easily identify with people who are perfectly content to live and work in haphazard settings. I realize that I may not have grown to be this insistent about my personal surroundings without the influence of my own upbringing, naturally, yet I have also come to discover a distinctive beauty and elegance to the concept of symmetry itself – specifically as it relates to a human's interactions with their environment.

At the same time, there is an interesting paradox of beauty insofar as the natural world is concerned.

Nature, of its own accord, has a certain gorgeous flair to its seemingly chaotic presentation. It doesn't have to be tidy to look beautiful. It just is. The sheer sense of unfolding growth, by its own accord, is elegance enough, and we're able to appreciate the visual beauty of this phenomenon without having to process it on a strictly intellectual level.

While the human form is also perfectly natural, there is a distinctive incongruence with nature that we have come to inherit in our learned behaviors and treatments of the world around us. We have grown to be "messy" creatures in many senses, and our refusal to remain connected with the natural world has only served to exacerbate this particular blemish even further. Through fears, infatuations, addictions and unresolved anger, we have found it easy to allow our minds to become morbidly obese in character. We have developed a cognitive, spiritual baseline in which we're weighed down by so much that we soon start to neglect the careful attention to the higher concepts and principles of our wider universe. We forget the Divine levity of nature itself. Our preoccupation with distraction gives us license to forego our deepest values in the face of stress or struggle, and we end up behaving and governing our lives in very messy and unclean ways.

This is why I value the importance of mindfully attending to the visual aspects of our personal surroundings. To observe the integrity of our personal space, and to dress our immediate, physical setting lends to a mindset of awareness to that which is outside of ourselves, as well as inspiring an overall appreciation for beauty itself. In my view, simplicity and restraint are very helpful elements in one's journey of consciousness.

At the same time, however, it is very easy for some of us (aka. *Brett Jordan*) to take this to the extreme of escaping into estheticism itself – which only becomes another form of distraction, not to mention serving as an artificial way of covering up the other messes of our lives, and essentially that of our hearts. To be sure, there are many beautiful homes in this world, with stunning apparitions of order and cleanliness. Yet a surprising number of these dwellings are nothing more than thinly-veiled coverings for a much deeper, more insidious form of chaos and dis-ease. In many homes, unfortunately, the picture one sees is a careful illusion, and the painstaking efforts to run a picturesque house is nothing more than a knee-jerk attempt to control what is in the *outer* world, while the inner one remains in a persistent state of turmoil.

Personally, I am no stranger to the latter pathology, and it is something I've had to wrestle with in my own life. That being said, I have come to appreciate the unspoken balance in these things, and that the moment I find myself needing to justify or enforce having a clean house is the very same moment I am no longer secure about something within my *inner* self.

The point is that tidying one's physical environment is never a replacement for the ordering of one's heart and mind. It will forever only be window-dressing if that's what we're trying to do. And while bringing beauty into your life is certainly a healthy and advisable thing, it is by no means the singular remedying tonic to one's pre-existing disorder. And perhaps this is something I've only been able to really understand as a direct result of being a parent.

As you are likely aware, small children aren't exactly the most dedicated Feng Shui practitioners. At least mine aren't. The fact is, furniture is frequently pushed around, paint and art supplies pepper the floor, pictures are perpetually misaligned, no surface ever stays clean for longer than ten minutes, and dirty laundry seems to spill out of every nook and cranny like some kind of elusive cotton infestation.

121

It has not been unusual for me to come home from work and to be struck with the most stunning sense of visual disorientation. When our third child was born, the scene was rendered even more profound, as our newborn made it very clear that he could only be happy if he was being perpetually held in my wife's arms. *All day.* Naturally, whatever vain efforts we could undertake in staying on top of our kids' messes prior to baby's arrival was almost completely cancelled out, and our two older boys ended up graduating to an even greater degree of chaotic play as a result. After all, the nature of a messy environment is that it tends to breed even more disorder and flux.

It can be hard for a husband and father to fully grasp the sheer amount of work that a stay-at-home mom takes on every day. Mealtimes, alone, can be an achievement of mythological proportions (particularly when you've opted for a plant-based menu), and the domestic steps taken in between each of them can defy the imagination of most. Consequently, I have had to learn that a woman does not take loose appraisals very lightly – particularly when they're coming from a guy who hasn't had to deal with a single child's request all day and who has also had the luxury of spending the last eight hours communicating exclusively with beings who can actually be *reasoned* with. For that matter, I have also learned (the hard way, I might add) that a woman does not respond well to the seemingly-innocent question of "why does the house look like this?"

When it comes to life with kids, trying to stay on top of even the most basic of tasks has proven itself to be easier said than done. The fact is that many things just don't get done, period.

And somewhere along the way, we have to be okay with this.

A day in the life

In the tradition of always preferring an orderly home, naturally I've tended to gravitate towards an attitude of just ensuring that things are done and dealt with. It's no surprise, then, that in response to my request to pick up their toys that I hear my son Jacob's stunned reply: "but I thought *you* were going to clean it up."

My wife has had to convince me to accept the fact that our kids will almost certainly not follow through with the task of picking up their toys and art supplies unless one of us is literally right there with them, encouraging, reminding, redirecting and cueing at every turn (kind of like living with somebody with advanced dementia). So that's what I did today, after getting home from work. Resolving to just get things properly tidied up and the house looking halfway livable, I took the time to walk them through various cleanup tasks until we reached a satisfying point where I felt that the boys had absorbed a moderate bit of positive re-programming. This took a while, mind you, but we did it. Not the most fun for them, I'm sure, but at least it was peaceable and not forced. The point is that I really believe I'd be doing them a disservice by not enforcing some kind of accountability for the mess they create around the house.

I remember one occasion a few years ago in which I came home to find every single toy and artifact piled into a gigantic mountain in the downstairs playroom. Everything pulled out from their drawers (including the drawers themselves), figurines, musical instruments,

123

game pieces, stuffed animals, art supplies and books. If you ever saw the movie *Close Encounters of the Third Kind*, think of Richard Dreyfuss' character who, while in a manic state of UFO obsession, proceeded to build a literal landing site in his living room out of household garbage and mud from his backyard. Well, that's sort of how *this* felt. Items were bound ominously together with yards and yards of rope and string; interweaving through nooks and crannies of multiple objects like some devilishly-clownish rebar system. My efforts to comb my way through this labyrinth were further tormented by the growing realization that most of my attempts to unravel certain sections of the rope only seemed to induce greater tensions and knotting in more remote areas of the structure itself.

At any rate, I was naïve enough to spend the next 90 minutes of my life picking apart, extricating, and ultimately dismantling this horrid thing while my kids played happily upstairs without any cognizance whatsoever of what their dumbass of a father was doing on their behalf.

Never again.

Today, in particular, was basically a blur, partly because it was the last day of my work week, but also because I was feeling the effects of accumulated exhaustion in addition to the kids' energies being amped up to the max when I got home. Moving the kids through dinner, clean-up, and finally bedtime routine was a bit of a joke, to say the least, but at least my wife and I kept our outward displays of frustration within a controllable level. In other words, we raised our voices a number of times, but we didn't actually yell at our kids or throw them out the window. Not today, anyway.

One of the hardest aspects of the evening was the fact that my two older kids just seemed to want to scream a lot.

For Jacob, our middle child, everything was a trigger. Everything was just plain awful for him. It got to a point where, whenever we thought we had managed to transition beyond a momentary crisis with him in order to turn our attention to Asher's meltdowns, the house was instantly filled with the staccato shrieks of Jacob's grievances that our attention had unjustly shifted to his brother instead of him. Conversely, this did not help Asher's overall quest for our attention either, which only resulted in a more dramatic crescendo of wails, foot-stomping, and hostile accusations. My wife and I were very hungry, very tired, and very, very *done* with this level of energy that was clearly not going away any time soon.

Did I mention that the baby didn't want to be put down during this whole ordeal?

At one point my wife, in a supportive attempt to check-in, asked me how I was doing.

"I'm in hell," I replied solemnly.

Keeping true to my commitments, however, the evening concluded with Asher and I taking the time to lie on his bed and read some pages from one of his books. Lately he has been quite intoxicated by the Animal Ark series by Ben M. Baglio, so tonight's selection was *Hound at the Hospital.*

But something very unusual happened just as Asher and I were settling onto his bed. He did something that he has never done before, in all our years of our father-son bedtime routine. He looked at me as I lay collapsed lifelessly on his bed, and quietly suggested:

"Maybe we'll skip the reading tonight."

This woke me up instantly.

He wants to skip a book reading tonight? This was highly irregular and out of character for him. I mean, this kid *lives* on books. He devours them like candy, and he adores having us read with him - which is why my mind quickly went to a very guilty place when he said this. Had I really hurt him through some overly-obvious demonstration of how absolutely knackered I was over the course of the evening? Was he basically interpreting – perhaps for the first time in his life – that daddy secretly just wanted to take his exit from anything to do with kids tonight, and just stop being a parent?

I'll be honest. A strong part of me just wanted to accept his kind offer, give him a kiss, tuck him in, and leave the scene quietly. It was perfectly understandable. Well-deserved, even. Why not? After all, a parent needs to look after their own needs in order to effectively be the parent they need to be. And really, how consistent do I actually need to be? I mean, it's not like I'll be reading to him when he's 20 years old, right?

Exactly.

I won't be reading to him when he's 20 years old.

So what could I say?

"Tonight I really want to read with you," I told him.

So we read the book. And the refreshing surprise was that, in entering into this zone of simply choosing to be with my son, I again found that I was able to override the sheer fatigue that was pounding away at my every nerve. Somehow, my resolve to be mindfully present with my eight year-old child – despite the chaotic events of the day – was what helped and effectively refueled me to be a father and not simply a caregiver.

And the day ended well.

A tidying fast

At one point my obsession with having a tidy, ordered home had reached a point where I was exhausting myself on two different fronts. First, I would wear myself out from the endless task of picking things up from off the floor and putting things away. Secondly, I would deplete all of my mental and emotional resources in trying to encourage and facilitate my children to do this instead.

For whatever reason, having a home that appears consistently clean can easily become my priority if I allow it to, with everything else taking a backseat – particularly my full ability to be centered with my family. This led me one day to committing myself to a seven-day "fast" in which I would deliberately leave all clutter and mess around the house exactly as I found it. There would be exceptions, of course, simply for the sake of functionality (such as dishes, basic laundry and wiping the kitchen table), but on the whole I would not even touch the boys' bedrooms, their toys, their tousled bed sheets, or any craft supplies that were left on the floor. The contract I made with myself was simply that if I could not peacefully persuade my children to clean up after themselves, then I was not going to burden myself either. This would be my self-imposed program for seven days.

The result was that I ended feeling far more available and energetic for actually being with my children. Within about two days into this fast, I noticed that I could actually pay more attention to their little monologues, and felt generally freer to engage with them in a way that was remarkably free from feeling distracted or even threatened by any resistances that they brought forward. In this new state of *choosing* not to worry about the way the house looked, I could actually feel like a normal, healthy father. I simply felt more relaxed in my parenting.

For my own part, letting go of the picture of a tidy home has been one of my most unexpected educations, particularly because it has forced me to re-examine my priorities. The truth is that young children fundamentally need the emotional availability of their parents, and this availability becomes rapidly depleted when we give increasing amounts of attention to the physical contours of our homes, or any other aspect of our lives for that matter. Take it from me - an atypical sort of fellow who otherwise floridly shines in the areas of tidiness and mopping up – I can see very quickly how inaccessible I become to my children when I give too much of myself to this endeavor (and I know there will be *more* than enough time for me to straighten out bed sheet wrinkles once my kids have moved on in life). The point is that I will only ever have this particular *now* with my children, and I make a choice every single day as to whether I will squander it, or embrace it.

Growing up, I was raised to be very conscious of my messes and my play area. This meant that I was forever being instructed to clean up my room and to put away something the moment it was no longer being used. Again, not a bad thing to teach a child, yet in looking back, I also remember that I was not really permitted very much time to simply just be idle and free. Unless I was being instrumentally attentive to a specific brand of play or utility, moments of simply just free-flowing and zoning out really weren't encouraged. Maybe this is why I felt the need to daydream so much in school. Who knows? The point is that it became very difficult for me to grasp the concept of the moment for the sheer pleasure of what it truly is. For me, moments were abruptly bookended in elements of concrete time and objectives, and too much time spent just wondering inwardly was held suspect. A quick remedy to my daydreaming was the instant instruction to go and tidy or clean something. In all honesty, my favorite times as a child were when nobody else was around and I was free to simply journey into the quiet realm of the unknown. Unfortunately, however, these times were rare.

I mention this aspect of my childhood simply to illustrate the point that our children need a crucial amount of space to explore their relationship with the world around them. This is how they will discover themselves, and this is how they will find a sense of connection with their passions and natural curiosities. Over time, these curiosities – if given enough freedom to be entertained – will lead to mature and healthy expressions of their underlying nature.

Yet as with anything else, the seeking of balance is the mediating principle in this part of life. Without a mind for balance, we are at the mercy of extremes in our behavior, and in our impulses. We will either obsess over the house itself, or we will get so caught up in the private world of our children to the extent of an absence of healthy functioning *within* the house.

It should also be remembered that while we might normally prefer a visually tasteful environment, acquiring such should never be a prerequisite for the healthy flow of our mind. Some people simply can't concentrate or even process things in a functional manner unless their surroundings are adjusted in a very specific, or "spiritual" sort of way. In my opinion, this is just another type of bondage that we can easily tie ourselves down with, and it only serves to dissuade us from appreciating the sheer power of transcendence in all things. Religion, after all, can take many forms – including when our intrapersonal rituals become an inflexible dogma to us.

"Each one has to find his peace from within. And peace to be real must be unaffected by outside circumstances."
- Mahatma Gandhi

For myself, while I may always seek to refine my visual surroundings for as long as I live, I nevertheless continue to approach the embracing of the chaotic moment. I won't say that I've mastered the balance, mind you, but I pursue it nevertheless, and strive to forgive myself whenever I falter along the way. The guiding principle is simply that my children deserve a father who is keeping himself open to change, open to growth, and open to the collateral messes of their necessary and organic childhood spontaneity.

Don't fear whatever is happening

Generally speaking, for the past couple of years I have been in the practice of affectionately acknowledging my children in some fashion when they first get up in the morning. Borrowing from Gabor Maté and Gordon Neufeld's wisdom in their book *Hold on to Your Kids*, I have come to believe in the importance of deliberate, semi-ceremonial greetings with my children after notable periods of separation, such as after a night's sleep, coming home from work, or even after being out running a few errands. It's nothing elaborate; merely a purposeful, loving acknowledgment in order to underscore the connection. A back rub. An embrace. A kiss. In most cases, I feel that this practice is especially good for me as the parent in that it serves as a helpful reminder of the precious relationship that I want to maintain with my kids.

In all honesty, it would be very easy for me to just slip in and out of the house without taking any time or energy to connect with my children – chiefly for convenience' sake. The fact is, I'm a busy guy and hardly a day seems to go by where I'm not trying to efficiently move from one point to the next over the ensuing 16-hour period. But even our most well-meaning pursuits in life can easily become our greatest sources of bondage. Coincidentally, if we allow ourselves to lose our connection with our children because we're so preoccupied with the mechanical processes of providing for them, then will the subsequent tearing in our attachment be ultimately worth it?

In the simplest way I can say it, being a parent is no less about being in the *now* than it is for anybody else. In some senses, I would say that it's even more significantly so, probably because the training ground for mindfulness is much more rugged and raw when you're raising a child – yet the nature of the vocation itself pretty much requires you to be centered so as to do it properly and honorably, and not simply as a fad.

If we can pursue the path of mastering presence in the midst of raising a child, then we are pursuing a fine and noble journey, to be sure. Mastery will never be fully realized as a destination, mind you, but rather it rightfully remains as the spirit of the practice itself.

Being in the moment is, essentially, all that we really have at our disposal, after all. This is not anything new, as I'm sure you're well aware. To *want* the house to be cleaner does not make it cleaner, nor does *wanting* quieter children make them any less boisterous or loud. In addition, when we attempt to voice our frustration over the fact that the rooms are a mess, your child is not getting dressed to go out, or that the kids simply are not listening, all we're really doing is making a verbal response to our body's sense of pain as it relates to those things. There's an uncomfortable, physical reaction to what we're experiencing in the environment, and we respond impulsively by making it known to others.

In effect, the pain is driving you to react in some way, but usually the reaction only serves to compound the sense of stress even further; both in yourself as well as in others. The fact that your child may even seem to ignore your reaction is likely because they want to put as much distance as possible between themselves and the messiness of what you're bringing to the scene. They don't want anything to do with it. As a result, you are left holding an even bigger bag of anger than the one you started out with, and this will typically leave you with only one recourse.

You become *louder*, because they're not listening!

At moments like these, when the thought of taking a 'high road' approach seems impossible, just know that the overcoming of the monster that we sometimes become is actually *instantly* within reach. It's really that close, yet we often don't realize it – principally because we're too engaged in the flow of our anger and in trying to intellectualize it, or overthinking it. Despite the sheer wonder of our human brains, sometimes our most logical thoughts can be our greatest downfall.

This is why the most important response in any of these things is to just *pull back*. Paradoxically, it is both the hardest and the easiest thing for us. It's hard because we're so programmed and hardwired into reactive behavior as a species, and our natural inclination is to just stay the course of our impulses. Yet pulling back is so easy because – once we simply grant ourselves permission to let go of our customary beliefs about *right* and *wrong* – all we have to do is simply just release our grip in the absence of forced *thought*.

A quick tool is to simply notice the monster in the room (ie. your own ugly reactivity) and step aside from it. Allow for space to then enter into the environment. The beauty is that this is not about *adding* anything here. You are simply letting something go in the greater equation. Adding can be labor-intensive, and none of us need to be laborious during these highly-intense periods since we are already so depleted. Just make the choice to notice how you are being, and step away from it.

An integral part of being present and centered is to discern your own body's responses to stress, and to take the time to acknowledge these responses. This is why you need to stop what you're doing, and take a moment to pay attention to how your physical body is responding in the very instant in which you're feeling stressed. This act alone will have an incredible effect on helping to mitigate whatever is going on in your overly-reactive intellect.

Think about what's happening to you personally, in the heat of your stress. Ask yourself the following: am I feeling my heart rate increasing? Is my breathing becoming more shallow? Am I breathing faster? Am I having a sense of tunnel vision? Do I feel a physical pain somewhere in my body, such as my lower back or my head? How does the pitch of my voice sound?

Taking a moment to reflect and pay attention to these things does several things for us. First of all, it gets us back in line with our own sense of awareness and it helps alert us to the trauma that's happening in our personal systems. In this way, the trauma of the moment can become its own perfect alarm clock for our consciousness. And while "trauma" may sound like an overly dramatic word to use here, it perfectly captures the sense of internal violation that is going in some of these domestic moments. The fact is that this violation will have physiological repercussions over time if we allow it to, and may easily result in our default descent into brooding parenthood.

Obviously we are resilient creatures, yet we also have our limits and for this reason we need to take stock of how our bodies are behaving – especially since domestic dynamics tend to repeat themselves in families, and a repeat pattern of unhealthy response can easily lead to compromised health and wellness overall.

When 'trying' is not good enough

Our third child's birth was followed by several days' stay in the neonatal intensive care unit of our local hospital. My wife, thankfully, was able to stay at the hospital with our baby for this whole period, while I commuted to and from the hospital every day with our two older boys. Not a bad arrangement overall, yet times like this tend to bring with them complications of their own, naturally. For us, given my wife's struggles with generating a decent milk supply, it quickly became a priority to make sure I was consistently at the hospital at key times in between breastfeeding sessions in order to bring my wife her meals. At any rate, trying to manage my other two children's movements during this whole period became a medieval gauntlet in itself.

In the days that followed the welcoming of our newborn, Noah, into our home, I can honestly say that I had regressed into my former, highly-reactive version of myself, which I totally did not anticipate. After all, my expectation was that third time would be a charm, especially since, by this time, I was accustomed to the labor of having young boys around the house. I figured that I *had* this.

The problem was that I had allowed myself to become so negatively transformed by the experience of single-handedly managing everything else in our lives during that initial hospitalization period that I ended up becoming very unpleasant to be around. In fact, it actually took me a few *months* to come down from the hair-trigger stress reactions that I had developed while frantically trying to facilitate everybody's meals (without having to resort to fast food), to the point where I would find myself yelling at one or both of my older kids for even the slightest infractions.

Interestingly enough, despite my years of conscientiously 'working on myself,' my own ability to observe and become aware of my newly-developed behavior was still not enough to actually curb it. I kept assuming that I just needed some time to recover and that, given enough space, I would be back to my usual self.

Except that it wasn't happening. I was still reacting like that one awful schoolteacher that everybody remembers from their childhood, and my kids were doing very little to actually merit any of it, other than simply just being children. Somehow I just wasn't bouncing back like I thought I would, and it was actually starting to scare me. I remember reflecting to my wife on several occasions how much this felt like some kind of post-traumatic stress response.

The point is that part of my ability to eventually transition forward was through having to pay careful attention to my body's responses to even the slightest thing my older two boys were doing that seemed to annoy or threaten me...*which turned out to be a lot of things*. At any rate, it was not about any specific strategy or parenting technique as much as it was about simply turning the focus away from my children's behavior and allowing myself to focus on my own baggage instead. At some point during my newborn's arrival into the world I had somehow picked up this very big suitcase from off the luggage rack of my own histrionics, and for some reason I just couldn't put it down when I needed to.

My wife, God bless her, has always been the kind of partner who supported me in doing whatever I needed to do to take care of myself. In this case, her patience alone was a blessing that helped me find some space to get real and honest about how I was processing the trauma of my responses, and to take the time I needed to slowly work through it. Through this processing, I came to be convicted by one very simple, very basic principle.

Start by *stopping*.

A large part of my inability to stop myself from reacting harshly to my children was because of my belief that I was 'working' on stopping, instead of actually doing it! At the risk of sounding like a dispenser of B-grade, pop-psychology, I have to testify that there is little other reason for my being able to recover from this than by the frank act of choosing to stop reacting every time one of my kids did something to press my buttons. It meant having enough sense to grasp that I may very well still *feel* the sense of irritation rising up inside of me, but that any prospect of actually remaining decent and functional was through the act of simply just observing that immediate gut impulse of anger, and deliberately abstaining from reacting to it on an outward level. If there is any intellectual psychology to this, I'm afraid I'm not articulate enough to spell it out. If anything, I credit the success of it to the sheer power of *not* planning out the whole process; but by just walking it out instead.

Telling myself that I was going to refuse to react in a harsh way to my child was exactly the self-starter I needed. And the easiest part about it was that I didn't have to chain myself to some kind of tedious analysis and map it out. I didn't have to bore myself to death by trying to deconstruct it or "unpack" it. I just made a firm contract with myself and decided to live it. Once I got this, it was pretty amazing how quickly I was able to find a peaceful road out of the trauma-like experience I was dealing with, and it also led to an eventual ability to soberly reflect on what my mind had been doing to itself for months!

Children are always and forever going to be children, and this is the thing we often forget as parents. In our most heated and panicked moments we somehow adopt this insane demand that they become reasonable adults. Again, we do this singularly for *us* rather than for them. But it is a sure guarantee that losing your cool on a consistent basis is not the recipe for a peaceful domestic culture (least of all for your spouse).

It's worth re-emphasizing that a parent's greatest challenge is not in raising a child, but rather the raising of one's own awareness in the face of it all. It is through this latter exercise on the parent's part that the child finds a higher and freer space to grow, experience and ultimately become a healthier version of themselves. By contrast, when a parent is feeling routinely stressed or, at worst, threatened by a child's behavior, then it can become even harder for a child to find a healthy expression themselves. Instead, they will learn specifically how *not* to express, and will unconsciously develop traits and features in their complex personalities that will ultimately serve to inadvertently protect them and distract them, down the road, from the fullest exploration of their own selves. Not in every case, mind you, but certainly in many. And while it may sound as though swallowing one's anger could have detrimental effects of its own (ie. the repressing of natural emotions leading towards unhealthy and arguably even worse manifestations later on), the truth of my own personal experience demonstrated the opposite. This was because, quickly into the process, I discovered a distinctive sense of levity that had otherwise seemed very elusive to me. Being aware of one's anger and frustration and owning it is very different from sweeping it under the rug. It's what you *do* with the emotion that makes all the difference.

By simply just taking my over-hyped brain out of the equation, and instead just going through the lackluster mechanics of not responding to my body's fight response, I found that I was able to experience a certain dissolving of disdain and regret towards myself which had otherwise been a consistent part of the whole stress pattern.

Finally, eliminating any reason for guilt over my behavior turned out to be a very therapeutic experience,

139

and it served to reinforce my resolve to keep myself controlled and even-tempered. Quite frankly, my head could only get me so far in a case like this. It truly got to a point where I simply just had to robotically walk out the steps needed, let my big head take a back seat, and allow the unfamiliar dynamics themselves take the authoritative lead in retraining and re-coaching my intellect.

In other words, it was through surrendering myself to the reality of parenting's constantly uncharted frontier that I could once again appreciate the quiet art of exploration without needing to know the answers ahead of time.

If I may put it another way, I believe it is the art of honest curiosity that leads us to higher forms of behavior in almost every circumstance of life.

While we may not always realize it, we are guided by life's accumulative wisdom when we release ourselves to the freedom of being open to the chaos rather than unnecessarily fearful of it.

And kids are very good for teaching us that.

8

Exposing your own Oppression

"Nothing in the world is more dangerous than sincere ignorance and conscientious stupidity."

- Martin Luther King Jr.

As I have indicated earlier in this book, I have jokingly referred to myself as a *pathological* father.

When I say 'pathological,' I am referring to what I would call an almost compulsive tendency to experience the basic tenets of fatherhood in rather intense ways; beyond the norms of what I have observed in many of my peers.

By nature, I don't just worry about my kids. I get *frantic* for them. When it comes to missing them while I'm away, this sometimes morphs into an unprovoked sense of sorrowfully *longing* to be with them – even when I'm only gone for a few hours. Paradoxically, my periods of impatience with them can easily tip over into the realm of sheer psychological exhaustion, while my frustrations with them have been known to induce disabling degrees of disorientation and loss of focus. At the same time, my love for them feels like a profoundly-arresting, overwhelming wave of intoxicating warmth, and my physical affection towards them tends to be over-the-top, and somewhat circus-like at times. Finally, when it comes to contemplating my fathering, I tend to start philosophizing about it to unusual extremes (and then end up blogging about it).

As you can imagine, these extremes can easily wear a person out after a while. They're not sustainable, at least insofar as I've experienced, and are usually the furthest thing from a relaxing state of equilibrium.

Having been the sort of person who has always felt things on more intense levels, however, I would have to say that the extremes of my emotions, particularly in my parenting, has helped me to appreciate the value of a healthy balance; a centered positioning. Without having been able to go through the cycles of overwrought emotions repeatedly, and without the difficult experience of failing to find balance in the process so many times before, I believe I would not have been able to appreciate the gift of mindful centering as a caregiver in quite the same way. In many ways, I would say that this journey towards balance could only have come through my finally becoming a parent, and through having to face my own unhealthy extremes over the course of the very journey itself.

Granted, while having an overly-intense manner of reacting to things and experiencing my emotions can, at the very least, be regarded as authentic and honest, it goes without saying that such an extreme form of manifesting them cannot really be maintained over long periods, not to mention the fact that it can wear out your loved ones pretty quickly.

Prior to becoming a father I had very little concept of distilled, honest, self-reflection, and was really quite blind to the benefits of seeking a quiet wisdom in life. Instead, I was very much preoccupied with the glamor and the appearance of 'presentation.' For many years, my life was suffocated by the burdens of living externally from myself and of being too focused on the opinions and sensitivities of others. As such, I spent a good deal of my energies being focused on behavior that was expected of me, and very little time devoted to authentic examination of the status quo. I was, to a large extent, a product of conservative norms, and was the type of person who was carefully invested in portraying that role accordingly.

As a child, however, I remember being quite at ease with quiet reflection and daydreaming, and I was very much at home in the realm of my personal imagination. I enjoyed my solitude, and I did not see much attraction in pursuing a lot of social intercourse. My pursuits were largely solitary ones, yet I always liked and genuinely cared about people at the same time.

My parents were often bothered by this disposition, however, and felt inclined to position me in social intersections where I could 'come out of my shell,' so to speak, and grow out of my habitual shyness. It's funny how you don't really think about being "shy" until someone keeps telling you that that's precisely what you are. Consequently, I grew up becoming very conscious of this new identity as a shy person, and this carried with it the natural responsibility of needing to overcome it, or at the very least to manage it somehow. I think one of the most frequently uttered comments directed towards me by my parents was that I was so "antisocial." Again, I didn't realize that's what I supposedly was until I was educated, accordingly, and as a result felt inclined to begin mitigating something about the way that I was showing up to the world.

Essentially, the lesson I ingested was that the person I naturally *felt* like being was not acceptable, and therefore needed to change.

Over the following decades, I believe that I grew into a person who had lost something very precious that I had only been able to glimpse at for a few short years in my early youth. In the ensuing years, I remember having only a limited degree of access to personal, solitary free-association and, certainly, when I could feasibly get away with it, I would always retract into my solitude. Yet there was always that haranguing voice inside my head that kept insisting that I shouldn't be indulging in this particular pursuit. That it was somehow anathema to the more responsible course of normal development, and thereby something that needs to be checked. I think one of the major reasons for this was due to the imparting of a parental philosophy, at the earliest outset of my youth, that spending too much time in reflection leads to a certain vanity of thinking, and that no good can ultimately come from it.

Growing up in a rigid, exclusive religious sect was also one of the major sealants of this particular intrapersonal dogma. In the religious community that I came from, the very heart of humankind was considered to be the primordial engine of sin itself, and that any person who drew inspiration from the heart, therefore, was believed to be sadly deceived, and distastefully lost. While I can't accurately recount every nook and cranny of my developmental influences, I nevertheless suspect that these implanted ideals and values were to have a major impact on my ability to properly self-discern over the next few years, and that included the ability to mindfully observe the maiden voyage of my own parenting for that matter. Frankly, I was too busy defining and judging the outside world to be able to properly and soberly look inward at my own intimate thought processes and biases. In such circumstances, my growth could only progress in very specifically-finite ways, and the consciousness itself remained stagnant and unused, for the most part. If anything, the conscious part of me was a thing to be held suspect, and ultimately not trusted.

As a young adult, these mainstays in my persona had reached a point where I was altogether unsure of what to do with my moments of solitude, and inevitably found some addictive outlets to fill in the gaps quite nicely.

You can only be fake for so long

For myself, having a personal goal to be authentic and true with my own children was a big part of what helped me 'unschool' myself from the systematized, externalized and sterilized mechanics of my former worldview (and *self*-view for that matter). I think it came down to the basic fact that having a raw desire to become a healthier expression, or version, of myself brought with it the sharp necessity to examine my own personal imbalances. I simply just had to face these things, especially if I wanted to make sure I was imparting decent values to my kids while avoiding the transmission of unhealthy, inflexible dogmas. Growing

145

up within a fundamentalist context tends to emphasize *in*flexibility, and I knew fairly early on into my parenting that I did not want this type of inflexible thinking to be passed down to my child.

It also dawned on me that I could not feel right about the idea of predicting or attempting to predestinate the type of path my child would or should traverse for himself, nor could I stomach the thought of verbalizing my child's fixed personality on his behalf – well before it would ever have a chance to evolve naturally and organically on its own. After all, who am I to say what kind of person my child will become?

Yet I still had all these racing thoughts and worries that wouldn't go away. My heart was leaning in the right direction, but my actions revealed a well-worn programming that resonated far more loyal to the norms and beliefs that I was so desperately trying to move away from. What was I to do with all of these voices in my head? How was I to rid myself of all of the incessant noise – the very source of which was rooted in over four generations of dedicated, dogmatic observance? Consequently, the journey itself meant having to look very closely at not just my personal beliefs, but also my automatic methods and impulses for interacting with my environment; with the world, and the universe itself.

This is one of the reasons why *stillness* is so central to rebalancing and centering. Bringing the essence of stillness into the experience of a raw emotion is where true rehabilitation starts. It means giving yourself space enough to plainly observe the nature of the emotion, as well as your own physiological reaction to it, and to allow that space to bring you some clarity and perspective.

The concept of *space* in general is often elusive to us, as people, despite our current, trendy infatuation with the word itself. More often than not, in our workaday, hectic lives, we don't really know how to seek it out, let alone actually use it for our personal benefit. What tends to happen is that when we do take pause, our minds will usually go into some kind of recovery mode, though not necessarily a restorative one.

As mentioned earlier, there is a certain type of intrapersonal trauma associated with living in our post-industrial culture. This trauma is earmarked by countless social pressures, incessant adaptation to changes in our business and employment structures, deadlines and countless responsibilities that all serve to pull our attention away from our families, as well as our highest callings. One of the ways we debrief ourselves along the way is through the practice of mental distraction. At the very best, we find ways to recalibrate ourselves in order to reach a certain homeostasis of sorts; a stabilizing of our baseline aptitude for functioning in the environment around us. In many instances, this is all we need in order to resume our status quo level of function and go back to our requisite stations in life. For lack of a better example, we take a coffee break before our bodily systems get too full, after which we re-enter the fray of our social surroundings. Sometimes we may even perform better following these brief retreats, but they are generally used for *upkeep* purposes; not necessarily transformative ones.

There's nothing wrong with this, but it needs to be pointed out that the mere recharging of our batteries only has temporal benefits, at least insofar as being able to move through life at higher altitudes of awareness and peace.

Let me just ask you: are you genuinely satisfied with being able to maintain a status quo existence with your loved ones? Is it enough for you to merely have the energy needed to function "normally" at home, doing all the typical things that an acceptable householder does in our society? Alternatively, would you rather be tuning into a sincere path of personal growth that is filled with intellectual, spiritual and emotional exploration? For that matter, how much do you ultimately want to create a healthy environment of growth for your children as well? My suspicion is that you would truthfully choose these latter things, and that this is something you have already considered more than once in your lifetime as a parent.

The beauty of stillness is that it serves as a natural mediator between competing forces. When we release ourselves into it, it brings with itself the power to override our acute sensations of fear and dread, and it also systematically calms our impulsive fight, flight, and freeze responses. Stillness is the single most critical instrument in our capacity, as humans, to overcome the myriad stressors in our lives, not because it magically takes away all the bad things in our life, but simply because it provides a subtle and meaningful space between us and whatever is currently plaguing us. Furthermore, within that space we find the capacity to let all the coiled energies of negativity and hostility to slowly dissolve.

148

Think about it this way. Stillness (or quiet reflection, if you will) gives us the freedom to release all of our panic into a natural receptacle, or depository. It essentially works as a pressure valve that dispenses all of the angst and psychological energy that we've wrapped around various problems or situations in our life, thus allowing for a more sobered, clear picture of what we're actually dealing with.

It is so true that we, as reasoning creatures, like to form stories and meanings around everything in our environment. As such, we unconsciously and habitually give definition and form to virtually every little source of discomfort or pressure that comes our way. Without realizing it, by midday our amygdala has worked up a battery of meanings and negative associations about our environment, and our body has since begun laboring away like mad to respond, deal and navigate with all of the baggage that our brain has been cooking up.

But when we give ourselves a moment to stop *acting* and just sit quietly with ourselves in a secluded space, we will often notice a bombardment of thoughts, images, and various concerns swimming through our mind; like a sea of cognitive stimulants, all mixing and waxing into and away from each other. For many of us, we quickly feel even more discomfort, since this generally allows for the loosening up of some threatening things that we've carefully tucked away, out of our conscious periphery. Consequently, this is why some people have a difficult time with the practice of meditation. For them, it's either too disarming (brings up uncomfortable thoughts and memories) or it's too boring (it doesn't feed into their incessant, addictive need for distraction).

149

Yet when we allow the flow of stillness to unfold itself gradually in our mind, we will start to see that all of this cognitive and sensual litter that is cluttering our head is *already starting to be dealt with*!

It cannot be stressed enough that free-flow stillness is one of the greatest healers for emotional and psychological atherosclerosis. There is something about personalized free-association that serves a uniquely therapeutic role in cleansing the mind from things that have gotten persistently "stuck" in the various corners, caves and canyons of our being. If anything, this is nothing less than the basic process of allowing all of your carefully-crafted defense mechanisms to simply take a back seat so that everything else that's been suffocating can see the light of day, once and for all.

I recognize that some people might see this as a potentially dangerous exercise – particularly in situations where there is some considerable trauma that has been carefully buried and could therefore lead to further self-harm if brought to the surface prematurely. My response to this is that even the most brutal forms of psychological pain are healable, and that recovery from any degree of wreckage follows a similar, almost universalized course from inception to recovery. The point is that if we are sincere about our healing journey, then we really do need to allow our underlying fears and pains to see the light of day. These are the very things which, unless exposed to the air, will keep us in a perpetual state of developmental suffocation.

At the outset, eliminating the default coping mechanism itself is always the most difficult by far, whether it's an opiate or an emotional strategy of responding to problems in our life. The simple fact is that withdrawal from these things never feels very good. It is the point where we are the weakest, physically and emotionally, and where we are the most likely to retreat to the intoxicating elements that allow us to stay in a false sense of equilibrium. Putting it bluntly, we just want to go back to what's normal for us, even if it's the thing that's killing us the most. This is because the depraved things in life that are the most familiar to us are usually the hardest things to compete with.

Yet this is where the simple act of *trust* comes into play. The true quest for transformation in a person always needs to begin with one's adaptation to the realm of trust. Bottom line: few of us have all the answers to life's biggest questions. Yet despite our collective ignorance as a species, it is arguable that the brightest lights of humanity are those who passionately harbored a sense of unshakable optimism about their place in the universe – regardless of what their lives looked like, and irrespective of how difficult things were for them at any given time.

A remarkable example of this is found in the life of Harriet Tubman. Born around 1820, Harriet Tubman was an African-American woman who was raised in slavery, but who eventually escaped and spent the rest of her life freeing others from the same fate. She became a staunch humanitarian and abolitionist during the American Civil War, and ended up working as a scout for the United States Army. She led many rescue operations through the legendary Underground Railroad, and it's been said that not a single person died or was displaced during her rescue missions, despite the fact that these trips were fraught with the risk of death –

either by execution or simply by exposure to the elements. She was nicknamed the "Moses" of the Underground Railroad and, unfortunately, the most significant homage that has been attributed to her has been posthumous.

Yet, regardless of her delayed recognition in the pages of history Harriet was known for espousing a visceral and passionate belief in something that was ultimately greater than her own individuality. It was this vision of a larger, collective justice that helped fuel this electrical spirit that we read about in her.

Harriet once said that she *"grew up like a neglected weed – ignorant of liberty, having no experience of it."* I would speculate that this is a universal truth for so many of us – regardless of where we might be on the spectrum of oppression or 'captivity,' if you will. We don't resonate with liberty at our baseline thinking because, generally speaking, it's not part of our sensual or cognitive experiences. We just know what we know, and it's not until we venture to think outside of ourselves and outside of our current paradigm that we are then able to imagine an alternative future. Essentially, we're often stuck in this vortex of preaching liberty and social justice, and we openly show our disapproval for the state of our politics. Yet I would suggest that these are nothing more than just personal reflections of our own sense of imprisonment; the false perception that we really have little control over our place in these things.

For Harriet, once she got it in her head that freedom was a thing to be sought for and pursued, she made a choice. And partly what has made her life so legendary is the very fact that making this choice meant that she was leaving behind one type of struggle in order to pursue another type that would have no predictable features to it whatsoever. All she knew was that there was a freedom that could actually be attained, and it meant enough to her to reach for it. She once said quite plainly, *"there was one of two things I had a right to, liberty or death; if I could not have one, I would have the other."*

I think one of my favorite references to her early life was actually an anecdotal story about her mother. One of the cruelest elements of American slavery was that if you were a slave yourself and you had children, you never knew if you would even get to see your children grow up. They were considered your owner's property and could therefore be sold or traded at any time. As it happened, Harriet's mother gave birth to a son one day and, after having lost three of her other children already, she avowed that she was not going to lose this one as well. One day her owner announced that her son was, in fact, going to be sold to another landowner. But when that day came, and the men approached their small hut to apprehend the child, Harriet's mother emerged from the hut with an axe in her hand and promptly declared *"the first man that comes into my house, I will split his head open."* The report, we're told, is that the owner backed off.

Assuming that this part of the story is accurate, it would have clearly been a spirit like this that helped in shaping Harriet's earliest beliefs about the possibility of staring down your oppression. There's no doubt that taking such a stance was a dangerous thing to do, yet it beautifully underscores the hidden power that is available to us once we set the engine of our heart into a deliberate, committed pathway. In other words, freedom from this world's shackles is rooted in sincere determinism and the power of unbridled belief.

Now, I don't want to undermine or dismiss the horrors of individuals who find themselves in unspeakable situations that are beyond their control. Slavery and confinement are very real still today, and there are likewise toxic evils that many people are forced into against their will. So I'm not trying to sit over here in my cozy little privileged corner and say that all somebody has to do is simply step outside of their physical captivity, and just imagine that everything's going to work out perfectly. What I'm trying to point out is that there's a transcendent pathway to overcoming your internal captivity to something, to seeing beyond your personal interpretation of the "thing" itself. And I believe that when we do this, it carries a certain charge; a power-potential of bridging you into completely new circumstances that were otherwise not possible under your previously self-imposed chains.

To be clear, having a positive attitude may not necessarily or automatically overturn a bad situation all by itself. Yet having the insight to liberate yourself from the psychological *concept* of your limits carries with it an almost miraculous power to set in motion a series of circumstances, events and conditions that gradually, over time, can lead to great improvement overall in one's personal station in the world.

I believe it can be rightfully said that we each have our own dysfunctional pathologies in these temporal lifetimes of ours. Somewhere along the way in our path of making sense of the social world around us, we weave a tapestry of responses and beliefs that are unconsciously intended to protect us from harm. It is through these learned responses that we form an understanding of what it means to survive among other humans and we cannot help but cling to these formations. This is the fundamental story of the modern human. Yet in the very building of these formations we simultaneously erect the most impregnable prisons of our own oppression. We eventually find ourselves caught in these insidious devices, and when the more spiritual aspects of our being are finally allowed some space to reflect later in life – we start to see how fragmented we actually are. In too many cases we become sorely depressed and lethargic in our overall lust for life, though we don't really know why.

But the task of overcoming the oppression always has to start with overcoming your own construct of the captivity as it's been formed in your mind. In other words, how you've defined and internalized the situation is what will ultimately impact your fate, far more than the power of a gun or the condition of a disease or the policy of a government. This is why having an unbridled trust in one's most passionate ideas has always been the greatest threat to an oppressive system. And it is most emphatically true that we are our own worst oppressors. Consequently, we begin to threaten our fears in very healthy ways when we start to take physical, deliberate actions in life that go against the grain of what is the most familiar, or the most routine for us.

Yet if you trust in your journey, and if you are willing to release yourself to the fleeting discomfort of a transforming mind, you will surely find that the world itself begins to take on some very different proportions. Threat diminishes, and *hope* is restored once again.

But this can only happen when you take up the courage to look honestly inward.

Looking at you

Despite all our beliefs and opinions about our personal selves, it can be very hard for us to see our outward presentation through the eyes of another observer. For one thing, the 'other' of our shared collective can never really discern the intricate workings of our individual minds, which means that whatever understanding or concept we have of our own self will never be purely compatible or necessarily lined up with what others think they see in us.

Ironically, because our society is so obsessed with being *seen* in a certain way by other people, our subsequent definition of who we are often gets very mixed up, precisely because of how deeply invested we are in the opinions and customs of our surrounding communities. Furthermore, because our concept of *self* is often so colored by social influence (our compulsion to re-invent ourselves through the meaning-making devices of other people), the resulting 'self' that we are left with remains a very egoistic shell of a thing, and in no way reflects the much fuller, inner core of our true being.

If I can put it more simply, putting so much focus on our identity is - paradoxically - the very thing that will disrupt who we actually are, deep down inside. This is because *being* a developing person is so radically different from chasing the image of a so-called 'developed' person. As John O'Donohue described it, *"the ego is the false self-born out of fear and defensiveness."*

With that in mind, I find myself inspired and moved to continue travelling forward with this theme in my own life as a father and husband. It is truly a journey in which I am perpetually trying to better understand, navigate and master as I strive to reach higher ground with my children.

But I should clarify here when using the term "master." I'm not a believer in 'mastering' our children per se, nor do I believe that it's all about mastering the art of parenting itself, necessarily. Rather, the mastering in this context is merely the mastering of one's own self. It is the quiet ability to discern the steadily falling leaves of the maples, the elms and the poplars of our emotional intelligence, and to knowingly anticipate the blooming that comes in the aftermath of life's sluggish and dark winters. It is to perceive that life brings its own riches and nutrients when we need them the most, and that every difficulty is ripe with the opportunity for personal change and growth.

It is through this greater endeavor of trusting, of simply just knowing that life brings precisely what we need, that we inevitably bring the fuller and healthier versions of ourselves to the table of parenting, as well as to the overall table of social responsibility. True mastery is not found in asserting control over another being; but rather it is found in the overcoming of the temporal self so that one may sincerely serve and truly *love* another being. This is the love that comes with the maturity of discerning that the Winter of one's growth may possibly coincide with the Spring of someone else's. And this is perfectly okay.

Where the heart is

The greatest journey of a person's life is the journey of the heart.

With our bodies we traverse great physical distances; transcending both land and sea. Yet while we may cover wide swathes of this earth, connecting with diverse cultures and civilizations and all of their unique values and norms, it is nevertheless all too easy to simply view every one of our travels through the lens of our own concepts and beliefs. As such, we become the mere watcher rather than the keen *observer*. We become the visiting 'experiencer,' if you will, as opposed to the benefactor and the direct participant of wisdom itself. We become the glorified tourist who, by engaging merely as a consumer of novel experiences, end up cycling back to our routine station of life; having nothing more than interesting stories and anecdotes that speak of what other people in the world are doing, rather than re-imagining and refining what we could be doing within the fundamental theater of our own hearts and souls.

Similarly, with our minds we journey across the myriad, seemingly infinite territories of academic and cultural artifacts; amassing so much intellectual content in our heads that we consider ourselves informed. We call ourselves enlightened, even, simply because of the number of books that we've read or the amount of courses and workshops we've taken.   And with all our collecting of intellectual products, we end up becoming much too terrified to make any real stand or position in this world, simply because of our highly-educated obsession with being *reasoned* in our approach to the world's problems. As a consequence, our infatuation with level-headed decision-making leaves us tragically sterile in our ability to address pain, injustice and cruelty at the deepest levels.

Is it possible for the best-intentioned of us to watch a horror unfold, and to merely sit and passively watch it happening?

Not long ago I had a dream of an airplane crash. It was a devastating sight, seeing the large commercial airliner collapsing into the mountainside in the twilight of a late summer's night. In this dream I remember my immediate impulse to respond; to help in some way - even though I had little idea what kind of horror I was going to find up in that mountain. I quickly found myself gathering a crude assortment of 'rescue' tools from my home; hammer, rope, electrical tape, vinyl straps and several other miscellaneous things. My sole purpose here was to gather some kind of toolbox for my mission, and all I had time for was the materials that were immediately at my disposal.

But I wasn't alone, however, in having witnessed the devastation of the airliner. On my trek to the crash site I remember passing by a community hall at the very base of the mountain, filled with people whose primary purpose was to gather and form an organized, strategic response to the crash. As I watched from outside, I began to observe that the only thing these people seemed to be able to do was to discuss the disaster from varying angles and perspectives. The very decision on how exactly to respond to the passengers' plight was flooded with words, ideas, speculations and debates. As I watched this meeting unfold, I hesitated on whether I should be joining this group or not. After all, if I wanted to participate in answering a need as serious as this one, then surely the responsible thing would be to attend to the reasonable counsel of the experts. Such was not a time for naive efforts, or foolish assumptions, surely.

Yet I didn't do this. Instead, I took my leave of the meeting hall at the foot of the mountain and, with my childish collection of electrical tape and screwdrivers, proceeded to chart my own response to the suffering passengers who were waiting for somebody – anybody - to simply just show up.

True living begins with the quest of a pure heart. With such a heart we are able to penetrate through the distortions that have been established by civilized intentions, and we will somehow have the energy stores to press way further than our physical and intellectual selves would otherwise allow. This is because the heart is nothing less than our gateway into radical change in the earth, as well as fundamental change in our private lives. Spectacular as they might be, our cognitive thoughts may easily distract us from what we really need to do, in order to push us into doing what we believe we are *supposed* to do. And when we allow the primal limitations of the body, as well as the socially-constructed confines of the intellect to chart our course in life, then I guarantee you that there will always be a larger group of people who will suffer the loss of our true and most powerful ability to love, serve and inspire them.

But is the heart always right for that matter?

That's an even more interesting question, simply because contemporary wisdom would assert that, yes, the heart is most definitely the 'seat of the soul' insofar as the deepest issues of life are concerned. Without a doubt, today's contemporary sages give plenty of reason for looking to the heart as the single most important key in unlocking the fullness of one's destiny, and one could reasonably agree with these simple, beautiful revelations. After all, in our present age of increasing awareness about the mind-body connection and its implications for our health (whether for good or for evil) we can certainly understand and appreciate the critical role of our most mysterious and magical member and its capacity for cutting through the icy film of cold logic, and to take on the beautiful work of simply just embracing what is right and whole.

Yet despite all of this, there still remains some ancient indication that our heart is not necessarily as infallible in its secret estimation of things that we may believe it to be. We forget that it is still, after all, a vehicle. It is a part of the wider whole and thereby not the fullness of who we essentially *are* as expressed souls in this life. Not unlike our mind, the heart is a transistor for important content that is being messaged to us from energies and influences that are all around us; albeit at a much deeper level.

161

I would put it to you that we can still mistake the heart's language as unadulterated truth, and that - despite our enlightened efforts to break through the thick veneer of ego - we are still left with the very important task of setting our conscious selves in the flow of the highest morality. It goes without saying that there are many in this world who (unwittingly at times) position their hearts along toxic causeways and deceptive belief systems. They heap to themselves familiar customs and comfortable truths that already speak to their egoic desires and which, ultimately, leads them to regarding the private language of their hearts as sacred authority. Having embraced this personal conclusion in their hearts, they look no further. They perceive no deeper into themselves to examine the silent malignancy that yearns to stay secret...

Yet unfettered Wisdom is a river that flows naturally and organically through our world; through our universe. It is literally there for the taking, if we choose to take it. But along with that free will of choosing wisdom, we are equally endowed with the liberty of choosing a poisonous alternative.

"Does not wisdom cry? Does not understanding put forward her voice? She stands in the top of the high places, by the way in the places of the paths. She shouts out at the gates, at the entrance of the city, at the coming in at the doors." (Proverbs 8:1-3)

Paradoxically, foolishness uses a similar approach in speaking to our hearts, and this is given as a warning to us. We're told in the Hebrew Bible that foolishness and deception *"sit at the door of her house, on a seat in the high places of the city, to call passengers who go right on their ways: 'Whoso is simple, let him turn in hither.' And as for him without understanding, she says to him: 'Stolen waters are sweet, and bread eaten in secret is pleasant.'*

Does this mean that we are left to sort out this affair completely on our own? Without any recourse to a higher Intelligent influence on our personal charting through this life? Are we ultimately playing some high-stakes game of chance in which, at the end of the day, we're basically left to the mercy of a random outcome? If wisdom and deception are both calling out to our hearts with such profound voices of reason, then where does that leave us? After all, deep down inside we all have some very passionate desires and ambitions - but which ones are right for us? Is it possible to think that we've made an ethical, heart-driven decision about something, only to later learn that it was...well, wrong?

David writes *"search me, O God, and know my heart. Prove me, and know my thoughts. And see if there is any idolatrous way in me, and lead me in the way everlasting"* (Psalm 139:23-24).

Interestingly, the Hebrew Bible makes references to the human heart with both positive and negative connotations, which leads me to suspect that the heart itself - in spiritual terms at least - is not necessarily the singular or most ethical source of Wisdom, but rather is a principal *recipient* and benefactor of it. Truly, the heart can be Wisdom's passionate lover or, conversely, it can be its cancerous resistor. And this all depends on where we choose to align this mysterious organ. In essence, there are various wells to choose from, and our heart is the primordial vessel that we may freely lower into any one of those pools, at our own discretion. As David inferences, we are subject to bowing down to idols of

163

false concepts and convenient ideals, or of setting our clear sight on higher standards of living.

The book of Judges in the Bible tells us a story of the legendary warrior Gideon. Gideon's elite army of 300 men were selected among thousands of prospective fighters through an extremely simple screening process. When the scores of would-be soldiers were drinking down at the river, we're told that God took favor on the ones who didn't drink with their heads planted into the water (like dogs), but rather those who brought the water to their mouths with their hand. In other words, it was those who figuratively *observed* the water first who were fit for the battle. And while a lessening in numbers could be seen as a counter-intuitive approach in setting up a military defense against tens of thousands of hostile enemies, the indication is that the Divine seeks the *substance* of the heart for the highest task, while our ego seeks the mere consumption of everything else.

The secret to choosing wisdom is through the pursuit of *moral* wisdom itself. We are endowed with the blessing of prosperous decision-making when we simply make arrangements in our spirit to align ourselves with ethics and standards that speak of a vulnerable love and a desire to help build our world from the ground up. Alternatively, when we're seeking mainly the attributes of shallow achievement, such as amassing wealth for its own sake, collecting fancy credentials to make our intellect look bigger or even just being driven by nothing more than the slow death of a thousand fleeting pleasures, we actually find that we are killing ourselves.

Consequently, there ends up being many signs in our lives that will warn us of this poor pursuit of our human hearts.

Naturally, this extends to a wider, more global platform where more and more people are genuinely seeking a clear transparency within themselves. From the rooted place of the inner self, to the outward effect on the family and then ultimately to the greater community at large, the journey of the purified heart charts an entirely new course for human society. It is within the dynamic kernel of this one singular quest for purity that the trajectory of human civilization can become dramatically impacted for the better. Of course, it goes without saying that there will still be disagreements and colliding principles between people who are equally striving for moral justice, yet there is still the potential for quality fruit in conflicts such as these. This is because, ideally, when people are engaging together from individual places of authentic vulnerability and openness, the road to agreement becomes less paved with shallow distractions, and more focused on the elements of noble ideas.

So long as we are passionately pursuing the higher things of life - the service of others, the infectious mercy that overpowers every hateful exhibition, and the expression of pure love - then we can be assured that (stumble as we may at times) we will find ourselves increasingly being led by our heart's greatest music.

Every hateful and painful thing that we may assume is happening to us is nothing more than an amazing process whereby our heart is being given the opportunity to truly shine forth. The question is: what will be the actual expression of our heart, particularly during life's most challenging periods? This will ultimately depend on which wells we have chosen to immerse these highly influential organs. The heart, after all, does not speak from a vacuum, but from a far more dynamic realm.

"Above all else, guard your heart, for everything you do flows from it." (Proverbs 4:23)

With this in mind, let the heart find where it fundamentally needs to go. In the deepest recesses of our *discerning* hearts, the Divine is actually the one speaking through us.

Everything else is simply our own oppression.

9

The Pain that Refreshes

"Behind every beautiful thing, there's some kind of pain."

- Bob Dylan

What does a parent's pain mean for us, in the here and now?

I have come to see pain as something that is not without its own reason for being. It may feel random, inconsistent and even perverse when it shows up in our life, yet there's always a purpose for it. In the simplest way, pain can be viewed as that necessary guiding post that's there to help us in the path of our development as a caregiver.

Is pain natural? It is…and it's not. It's not natural in the sense that we're part of a beautiful universe that is designed to flow and expand, yet pain is also very natural as a consequence of premature disruptions to this expansion and growth. Pain is usually the result of something disruptive in our human experience, and yet it's also there to serve as a natural effect of the things that we often do when we're being ignorant to the path we should be following. Similarly, it comes when we've ignored something very important in our lives; or even when our antecedent generations have ignored

167

something profound, leaving us to work out the balance in our own lives. As the expansive insight of the Divine was pointed out to Moses;

"I am a God without rival, allowing a man's depravity to reach his own descendants…and yet I reveal goodness to the ones who endorse love" (Exodus 20:5-6).

Either way, when we interrupt our own cognitive and spiritual expansion by clinging to anything in particular, we are definitely going to be subject to pain. This is simply because the act of pursuing or in simply trying to maintain a fixed status quo, be it money, security or stability, will necessarily involve the lingering possibility that these things might not ever actually be secured, or that they might be lost one day. Unsurprisingly, this sort of preoccupation will tend to manifest in psychological rigidness as well as possibly leading to various medical problems and chronic illnesses – merely because of the severe hit that our physiology takes as a result of this sorry marathon. Simply put, we keep ourselves spiritually chained and stunted whenever we fixate on anything that exists merely in form, when we should instead be checking such impulses in favor of quietly trusting that all will work out in our life so long as we are consistent and faithful in our deepest values.

Problems will come to us, no doubt about it. Regardless of how "on track" we are in life, there is no person who has been endowed with the real-life fantasy of a trouble-free existence. Yet, regardless of their origin, it is these very troubles that are the key milestones in our developmental journey, particularly insofar as a growing family is concerned.

I think that Barbara Marx Hubbard captured it very well when she said that *"we need to see current problems as evolutionary drivers; as crises requiring us to innovate and transform in every field."* In this way, problems can serve as unexpected charioteers in humanity's honest progress, though perhaps more so when it comes to our psycho-spiritual *perception* of a situation and the resulting wisdom that is acquired in the process, rather than on the concrete nature of the difficulty itself. After all, there is no lasting potency in a problem once we look inward for the answer.

My wife, bless her heart, has had to remind me more times than I care to remember that I tend to ask why my child behaves a certain way – when I should instead be asking what I'm supposed to be learning from the behavior itself. Or more specifically, what I need to be learning about *myself* in direct response to that behavior.

The emphasis ultimately has to be on where we're going to let problems take us. Viktor Frankl, the Holocaust-era psychiatrist who pioneered the practice of logotherapy, saw the transformative power of finding meaning in problems and in suffering, and specifically for the purpose of healing and development. But this shouldn't be mistaken for attaching judgment to a situation, necessarily. You see, we can look at a painful situation as being some kind of cosmic punishment or moral retribution for being a bad person, or we can instead reframe that pain; thereby recognizing it as an intervention of sorts. In other words, we can see the pain as a condition that is interceding for us as a result of a thought pattern or a behavioral cycle that hasn't been working, and so it's calling us to examine ourselves and to work out a progressive path for new development. For that matter, sometimes the pain is simply there to steer a person back to what is fundamentally of greatest value to them.

Plainly, it can be seen as an opportunity in disguise. As we have seen, there are certain members of the human race who allowed themselves the liberty of simply facing their anguish; who took the time to process the experience of it in order to draw out a better self. A fuller humanity, even. If we didn't have these examples, these pioneers who go before the majority, I personally think that our collective body of spiritual wisdom would be significantly lessened. In this way, I think my world is that much better because someone like Nelson Mandela made three decades of prison first break him, and then rebuild him.

We are navigating not merely the current incarnation of our lives but also our shared collective existence of them, and we're ultimately in this together. Beginning with our families. With this in mind, there are many exercises we can incorporate in our life that not only help us to identify the roots of some of our deepest problems, but that also help us find pathways out of the thought patterns that keep us victimized.

The world of Integrative Medicine draws heavily on what we call 'yogic cognitive-behavioral practices.' But for our purpose, we'll just say "mindfulness practices." These can include things like meditation, Qigong, Tai Chi and various breathing exercises, among other things. I would certainly include prayer in this list, with the understanding that even prayer itself can be used in many ways, and for various aspects of awakening, detoxification, and renewal (all of which are conducive to the ultimate goal of reconnecting with Higher Consciousness). I would also draw attention to the newly-emerging discovery of Ho'oponopono, a Hawaiian-based healing practice that incorporates meditational forgiveness and gratitude as a way of reaching higher states of being.

Regardless of which practice you're adopting, mindfulness exercises are amazing things that help to restore mind-body holism, and they've been shown to be very instrumental in recovery from physical disease as well as various mental illnesses. A fascinating review in a 2012 issue of the *Asian Journal of Psychiatry* demonstrated how mindfulness exercises actually have a positive effect on the process of human gene expression; even to the point of influencing the messenger molecules that convey information directly from the DNA itself. I'm not a physicist, mind you, but my understanding is that these messenger molecules are part of the first step in the constant engineering of our genetic makeup, and that this process can actually be nurtured by the deliberate act of mindfulness. This finding is also very compatible with the emerging science of epigenetics; the idea that our internal response to our environment is actually more significant than our inherited genes (which is very controversial for the reason that people often like to hide behind their genetics).

Pointedly, the data raised in the article suggests that practices such as these have a potential to *"exert beneficial effects on immunity, metabolic rate, and apoptosis through modulating gene expression"* (Saatcioglu, 2012, p. 75). The word "apoptosis" (yes, I had to look it up) basically refers to the process in which certain cells die out as a natural and regulated part of normal, developmental growth. This type of cellular death is different from necrosis (unnatural cellular death), in that it is often regarded as a pre-programmed aspect of healthy growth that we actually want to see in our bodies. Without proper apoptosis, we would be subject to various degrees of gene mutations.

In other words, we are seeing that yogic practices have a direct impact on our own physiology. These timeless exercises actually serve to enhance the natural growth patterns in humans, thereby augmenting human performance overall.

Even just conscious, controlled breathing over a certain amount of time has been shown to relieve the body of various toxins and illnesses; not to mention inducing higher levels of cognitive functioning. And the thing about our thought patterns is that they can either be a blessing or a curse, depending on what we do with them. They can break us without remorse, or they can be the greatest tool of repair that we have. The *Asian Journal of Psychiatry* also points out that it's not so much the specific method that you're using that can make a difference, but rather that you're using some kind of mindfulness practice at all, and that you're bringing this into your life on a consistent, deliberate basis. Ultimately, *"regardless of the method employed, (mindfulness practices) can give rise to basal gene expression changes..."* (p. 76). Essentially, the point is that being mindful is part of a dramatic transformative process, both biologically as well as spiritually.

Yet, despite these proven facts, most of us struggle to find the wherewithal to actually implement these tools into our daily lives. Distraction and preoccupation from life are the thieves that rob us of our true potential as enhanced human beings. Distraction from our lives and distraction from our deepest thinking is the drug that will keep us tethered to the withered pole of mediocrity, and I would lovingly suggest to you that we live in a culture where the false sensation of a mind shift is simply just through the stroke of a keyboard. One mouse-click, and we very easily rob ourselves of several hours of actually being able to honestly process our level of satisfaction with life; not to mention the sacrifices we make in terms of actually educating ourselves and forging new paths forward in our cognitive and spiritual processing.

If I can share anything that I feel is worthwhile here, it would be to emphasize the singular value of investing in our spiritual and mindful wellness. This is something that is critically important as we are increasingly bombarded by tools and options that promise us fixes and solutions for our fatigue, our strain, and especially our pain. Without a doubt, our healthiest spiritual expression is rooted in how we are able to awaken ourselves; or more appropriately, how we are able to *be* awakened in this life. One of the key ways that we open ourselves to this is by being willing to face who we are inside, and to examine our beliefs as honestly as we can.

But if I can put it more bluntly, the key to building a meaningful existence is by directly facing whatever pain is living inside us. Naturally, it goes without saying that the practice of meditation can be a fantastic tool in this process.

I get the fact that meditation is something that gets a lot of play in popular culture - to the point of parody

173

sometimes – yet this does not contraindicate its proven track record as a powerful tool for centering. And while one could say that these are things that have become wildly hijacked and misappropriated in the Western world, the fact remains that there is an ancient wisdom in these practices that is compatible with most forms of spirituality. It seems that even the biblical King David himself was one who availed himself to elements of the practice, thus accounting for so many of the beautiful and universally-cherished Psalms we have in our possession today.

"O, how I love your words. They are my meditation throughout the day." (Psalm 119:97)

Now I'm certainly not a meditation teacher or any kind of sage when it comes to Eastern philosophies, but I do recognize the healing effects of them. And at the risk of causing offense to some of the more hardcore practitioners, I would advocate that any crude practice of mindfulness in our life is profoundly better than no practice at all. Again, the phenomenon of a changed life begins with a single act. When a single action is deliberately put into practice, the repetition of its unique quality will lead to mastery.

I'm going to keep this simple. What we're talking about is a willingness to face our thought patterns; to look at the way we think, and to be honest about why we fear the things we do. And the point is not to dwell on these things, necessarily, but rather to understand the condition of our baseline; the way we are functioning right now in our immediate family, social and spiritual environment. The task here is to ask ourselves, "how did I end up here? Why do I believe the way that I do?"

174

And it's from this place of awareness about ourselves that we then continue with the journey of our destiny. The adventure of our lifetime. It was T.S. Eliot who said that *"we shall not cease from exploration, and the end of all our exploring will be to arrive where we started and to know the place for the first time."*

I would put it to you that our greatest and most profound journey through this life comes with being able to face our own programming, and to put in the work of actually re-programming ourselves in a way that is more authentic to who we actually are. Every day we may show up to the game of life with our own ideas about what our identity is (again, 'identity' is something that we have become quite infatuated with in our modern culture). But all too often, what we have clung to as our identity often has more to do with our ego than anything else. And the ego is nothing more than what we've inherited as a result of our experiences, our influences, and the after-effects of all the pain we've ever experienced – and the subsequent walls and weapons that we've developed as a response to those things.

I'll be honest. Sometimes trauma will surface during these mindful exposures. I've met people who discredit meditation simply because, for them, it has led to some rather uncomfortable experiences. But the point is that sometimes we are going to be uncomfortable or surprised by the thoughts that come up when we allow ourselves to visit the internal machinations of our socialized being. But if we can just allow ourselves the gift of actually facing these things, we will surely find a refreshing opening in ourselves that ultimately transcends all of the emotional and psychological baggage that we've been carrying around with us.

175

Facing discomfort as a parent

When it comes to parenting a child, the experience of a caregiver can be so unique in the way that it thrusts you mercilessly into the psychological vortex of facing the things that you were once programmed to be afraid of. More often than not, unfortunately, we end up digging our heels in and we refuse to acknowledge the learned baggage that is directly calling the shots in our dysfunctional parenting responses. In some senses, it's like our impulsive reactions to our children are either automatically in tandem with what we learned from our own parents, or they are carried out in a desperate attempt to avoid being like them at all costs.

But if we can somehow arrest the moment of our parenting stress – the moment where we are frantically trying to get our point across to our child – and reflect on some of the possible roots of our reaction, I believe we will uncover some interesting surprises. Granted, it is often no easy task to pull ourselves out of an acute situation in the family dynamic, and we need to go easy on ourselves when we end up taking the lower road in these interactions. In this case, take the time to revisit and reconsider the details of the incident that took place between you and your child, and let yourself become vulnerable to the facts of what happened – and not your beliefs about how it should have played out.

Easier said than done? I challenge you to do it anyway.

The only other choice is to simply remain angry and stressed about your child's behavior, and to fume about the fact that they were so insolent and difficult. Sadly, this is the plight of far too many parents, and I would be lying if I said that it isn't something I still have to navigate in my own parenting from time to time. This is why it cannot be emphasized enough: while firm boundaries have an important place in raising children, our kids are far better served when their mother or father has enough insight to examine their own side of the conflict dynamic, and to be willing to actually explore some of the underlying roots of why some of the parent's own emotions were so sharp.

"It is not by muscle, speed, or physical dexterity that great things are achieved, but by reflection, force of character, and judgment." (Marcus Tullius Cicero)

With a doubt, mindful reflection into yourself involves plainly examining our most unwanted and discomforting thoughts and emotions; recognizing that they are simply the things in life that we have not dealt with yet. They are still dormant in our psyche, and the very fact that they are so quickly accessible within a meditative state shows us, ironically, how much of a role they're actually still playing in our life. And this is precisely why it's good to acknowledge them, so we can cleanse ourselves – progressively – through a change process that's organic and natural. Because it's either this or the myriad other mechanisms that society is dishing out to us in order to induce a plastic change; a temporal relief from that irksome feeling that something just isn't working for us.

Plainly speaking, our baggage will forever and always be the master of us so long as we refuse to open it up and expose it. Otherwise, the very nature of parenting itself will keep probing us to look at it, no matter how much we try to resist it. And that's the great thing about the occupation of parenting itself. It just has this fantastic way of beating us down repeatedly until we finally just recognize a few things about ourselves that need to be addressed. It's when we take the bold leap into the unknown that parenting actually starts to become an amazing journey for us, and no longer the marathon of psychological drudgery that it is for many. In effect, our children can be our greatest assets in fostering this pathway, and when respected as such they will undoubtedly find their own moral compass in the process.

Essentially, pain and discomfort can be great tools for us. They can be the things that help generate the enrichment and fermenting of our character, and they can serve as healthy triggers for new direction. It should also be pointed out that if we don't start addressing the disruptions in our person and instead ignore the things that are separating us from connecting with our highest ideals, we end up in a repeating cycle where we keep choosing the things that just aren't helpful to us. Furthermore, we play into an even larger societal trend of choosing distraction so as not to deal with some of the wider-scale pain and injustices that are still very much a part of our overall civilization.

Finally, I would suggest that our collective spiritual wellbeing, as a species, is a singular vital link in the overall chain of humanity's progression. This goes hand in hand with the principle that the future of our progress on this planet is closely linked with the way that we treat each other, and it is a potent fact that the way we forge our own sense of human responsibility will surely lead to greater, more resilient partnerships in our communities and, by extension, across entire nations.

Additionally, our embracing of personal responsibility is sure to bring a substantial currency in dissolving the manufactured turbulence that others in this world are facing.

This is why true social development (mindful development) can begin with where you are in your parenting. Your willingness to grow into your higher self (the very self that was destined in the image of God) will not only be of benefit to you personally, but more importantly to a wider family of human beings who are collectively in search of progress.

To borrow a much overused concept from Gandhi, we need to be the progress that we want to see in our world. We hear it all the time, yes, but its wisdom has far from faded.

10

The Cornerstone

"If a man does not keep pace with his companions, perhaps it is because he hears a different drummer. Let him step to the music he hears, however measured or far away."

– Henry David Thoreau

Some people make a decision not to have children. I would never presume to analyze someone's reason for making this choice, primarily since the only person's shoes I have ever walked in are my own.

At the same token, my suspicion is that there are a disproportionately large number of couples who make the choice not to start a family for no other reason than simply just fear of the unknown. One of the most common reasons I hear from people is that it sounds like so much work to be a parent, or the perception of there being not enough support from family or community in order to pull it off successfully.

Without a doubt, community is a very important part of family life. It can often provide a value-driven backbone to the individual household itself, while also acting as a supportive agency in a variety of ways. Community can augment a family's resources, intervene during times of crisis and emergency, and even serve to give solid counsel in periods of moral distress and disorientation. Furthermore, a morally-cognizant community can act as a great reinforcement to a family's established values and principles, ultimately serving to secure a child's sense of attachment to their parents and their chosen ways of life.

Yet it's very true that communities like this aren't necessarily found in every neighborhood, and this particular definition of it is often all-too ideally painted.

The reality is that one's pre-ordained community (aka. the "village") is not necessarily the utopian, mutually-invested ecosystem that we typically wish it to be. Certainly, there is something to be said about intimate faith-based groups and traditional social networks, as well as communities and neighborhood hubs that are founded upon shared values and ethics. Yet my sense is that many of us assume that a pre-established community or collective agency needs to be already at our disposal in order for us to even consider a safe program of family-planning. In other words, we figure that without a concrete church, synagogue, mosque or flourishing cul-de-sac already laid out for us – we are subject to a barren landscape of childrearing without any social tools or cultural resources whatsoever. For that matter, if our parents don't live within a 50-mile radius, or if all the cousins live on the East Coast and we're living on the West Coast, the fear is that we're basically planning a suicide mission by getting pregnant.

But there's a well-guarded secret that lurks beneath the intimidating, socially-engineered infrastructures that tower all around us. A secret which begs to be exposed and embraced in its capacity to set our families free from

182

all of the crippling fetters that earmark our dependence on the status quo.

This unspoken truth is that an authentic community actually begins with *us;* the individual family.

We are the cornerstone of the ethical and social edifice we desire for our family. The moment we forget this principle is the very same moment that we are tempted and allured by the easy and well-worn paths of the social norms that stream all around us, effectively downgrading our values and beliefs in order to fit into a group or culture that is essentially foreign to our deepest selves. We surrender to something that takes away from our family rather than actually gives anything of value to it. And through this surrendering of our honest values to the stunted norms of urban civilization, we end up falling prey to that most insidious of diseases: civil apathy.

Among other things, civil apathy is earmarked by a stunning absence of curiosity within a community. The members are simply too worn down by the sheer lassitude of living by the collective standards of everyone else that it becomes consistently unlikely that anybody will actually question some of the group's deepest ethics and goals for themselves. Furthermore, it is symptomized by a culture of individuals who are not in touch with their truest nature and who therefore feel the need to be legitimized by those around them. In this sense, it is only too comfortable to present one's self as part of the wider group - though we nevertheless appease our innate craving for alternative values of deeper meaning by tattooing ourselves with decorative Asian symbols and words, wearing chains with Buddha pendants, or signing up for yoga classes (I was recently struck by the sight of a sadly enervated, tired-looking woman wearing a T-shirt that said *Free Spirit*). The fact is, deep down inside we actually know that something isn't lined up properly within our personal, existential frame. We long for meaning and expression of something very profound, yet it strangely eludes us on account of our distracted and numbed senses.

As it happens, however, the family dynamic can once again play a pivotal role in reformatting our relationship with life itself. This is because the most potent seeds of change are found in the very heart of a family's unique intensity, and likewise in that family's lusty courage to step beyond the confines of what is deemed acceptable to all others.

Without a doubt, one family's ability to hold their own against the tide of popular living prescriptions around them is what actually lays the groundwork for true, holistic community (and society itself, for that matter). Furthermore, it is the family that has the courage to pursue its own path that sets a precedent for authentic living, and it is precisely this family which – by its very boldness to trek its own way – naturally causes other families and individuals to gravitate towards it. This is because we live in a society that is utterly saturated with inauthentic ways of living; of being with one another in every which way other than organically relating. Consequently, any party or agency that is standing in quiet resistance to this plastic tsunami of human noise will necessarily draw some attention over time, and it goes without saying that those individuals and families who are guided by a deeply-set need for true living will be curious to know more about the families that are pioneering healthier roads in our world. In effect, it is through this slow and finely-fermenting fashion that relationships are born and true communities are gradually cultivated.

I want to carefully point out that I'm not advocating for just being a hermit family that doesn't want anything to do with other people. Nor am I in the least way promoting that the healthiest families are basically mini cults. At the risk of encouraging even more division in our fragmented society, I'm simply saying that community is essentially what we make it. The integrity and overall health of a hub of people depends entirely on the value-driven makeup of the individuals themselves. By contrast, placing undue emphasis on the group cluster itself (the agency, if you will) we end up surrendering our essential humanity to an over-arching system that serves to 'organize' rather than actually serve its members. This is why the healthiest brand of community is one that is made up of perpetual founders, as opposed to perpetually-passive members. The most centered type of community, for that matter, is one whose participants recognize the importance of co-leadership, rather than being caught up in co-dependence.

On a personal note, my wife and I struggled for several years following our exit from a deeply-entrenched religious community. For myself, being a fourth-generation member of our exclusive sect meant that, by leaving, I was basically cutting myself off from the closest and deepest human connections that I ever knew. Even some of our family's financial security became arguably at risk upon making our choice to resign from the community we both grew up in, and I'd be lying if I said that I did not feel highly vulnerable at various periods in the wake of our emergence. Yet if we had stayed with what was merely comfortable and familiar to us, we would not have grown in the way that we did, and we would not have been able to give our children the experiences and the lessons that we knew we wanted to give them.

It ultimately meant searching out a whole new frontier at a time when we didn't even fully know what we were looking for. All we knew was that a better, healthier and more meaningful road lay yet to be explored, and the longer we remained committed to the values and beliefs of our pre-ordained community, the more we were sacrificing our deepest values as a result. The more we were dying, really.

But I digress.

I share this personal glimpse into our lives simply to make the point that sometimes our best destinations in life are the ones that we're simply not familiar with. This is why it is within the silent spaces of our most naked contemplation that we begin to perceive the best path forward for our lives, and often these paths won't always line up neatly with standard rationale or social logic.

Yet, at the same time, we can see that society itself is changing as well. We are living in an age where concepts of personal transformation and social transcendence are increasingly valued, as is the idea of taking courageous risks in order to live a life that is more in keeping with your highest calling. Simultaneously, it can be argued that older, archaic principles of investing exclusively in 'security' and focusing on linear models of family-planning are gradually ebbing away. We are effectively watching the tide of our pre-baby boom generation drawing back out to the primordial sea of behavioral evolution, and are consequently witnessing a new earth of possibilities becoming clearer before us. To be sure, there have always been a few members of our species that have grasped the wisdom of personal revelation, but it seems that now we are living in a time that is very ripe indeed for a larger number of people on the planet to embrace revelation as well. The revelation of awakening.

Classical, religious concepts of future revelation and cosmic 'judgment,' I would argue, are nothing more than crystallized and altogether halted interpretations of a much larger, more fuller reality of a universe that is persistently and eternally unfolding. To say that the Divine manifestation through the phenomenon of our species can only be played out in fixed, abrupt leaps is to deny the perfect beauty of a Divine Consciousness; a Consciousness that is always, perpetually there in the first place. To be sure, we are on a road of discovery, and there is so much we do not know – nor can we possibly know - within the narrow confines of a single lifetime. Yet we are endowed - anointed even – to fundamentally *be here in this moment* and to set our finest instruments of human intelligence to witness, reflect and be shaped by the adventure of this lifelong discovery. In due time, we will see our consciousness ascending to greater heights of virtue, yet all of this takes time.

In this way, 'the rose will bloom in a desert place,' as the Hebrew scriptures put it, but this does not happen in a vacuum. There still needs to be a conscious, deliberate seed to begin with, just as there needs to be fertile soil for that rose to take root, and also the presence of a sower – an active, voluntary agent – to do the sowing itself. I would suggest that this is the very purpose of humanity. It is to be willingly involved and receptive to what is revealed in the process of waking up to timeless wisdom; timeless ethics of Divine morality and profound truth.

And 'truth,' for the record, is not a bad word.

We must never fear the concept of it. It does exist, even though we may not understand it. Our popular apprehension in talking about what's "true" comes through the fear of boxing it in, capturing it and suffocating it through definition and words. And through fear we either cling to rigid interpretations of it or we shy away from even talking about it for paranoia of seeming naïve or grossly uneducated in the eyes of others.

Yet truth is always there, and it is permeated in everything we could ever experience in our lives. Truth, as a wise and honest emperor, is consistently at work in the greater expanse of our existence, and it is forever in favor of a curious humanity. Furthermore, it does not care in the least if we have only a partial understanding of it. It simply just is, and always will be – whether we hear its language or not.

This is why humanity has been allowed to flourish in the first place. Not to advocate on behalf of truth like some kind of proselytizing agency, but to actually live it out in the fundamental expression of our existence. The question is: are we listening? Are we really listening with our deepest, most curious selves? Have we sincerely been able to tap into the innocent and blatantly non-egotistical curiosity of a child? Or, like most of the people around us, have we allowed the cult of personality and forged identity to cloud our finest receptors to intrinsic wonder?

Maybe this is the real reason why our job has always been to take care of the children in our lives. Maybe it's through the utter transparency of an enquiring child that we are invited to re-examine our own blinders and beliefs; to openly perceive the fabricated layering of our false selves – the layering which we have unwittingly clothed ourselves with in order to survive the unpleasant things we've come to believe about the world.

This is why the child challenges us, and why the child essentially *exposes* us. Sometimes my own child will simply ask the question "why do you believe that?" and I am left dumbfounded, with no recourse other than to defend my ignorance or to surrender myself completely in that naked moment of opportunity. In essence, that is the moment in which I am divinely invited to perceive at a much deeper level, and am thankfully reminded of the fact that so often I am vacationing in the mere shallows of life when I should instead be journeying in the far richer depths of it.

Real living, after all, does not happen in the shallows.

This is why I believe that we need to be striving, continually, in order to release ourselves into the amazing chasm of honest reflection, despite the fact that it doesn't come easily at times. Regardless of the positive changing tides in our social awareness, we are still struggling as a civilization and we have a ways to go yet. We still care way too much about what others think of us, and we continue to wrestle with the idea of being completely honest with our own selves.

To put it simply, we are still at odds with the acute moment of *now*; whether to be at peace with it completely, or to embrace it without feeling the impulse to race to the 'next' moment in order to get away from this one. And when this trend becomes entrenched as our life's roadmap, we are automatically addicted to convenience so that the now is made more palatable; easier to swallow.

To take it even further, we are educated enough to recognize the ways in which our race has been a straining presence for our planet, but there is still a substantial disconnect that is keeping us from actually changing our environmental behavior on a wholesale level.

In many ways, then, human consciousness enters into this world in the form of a child. And children, by their very nature, ask questions and poke holes in what they see. This is a necessary phenomenon for us. It's something we need to be grateful for.

For this reason alone, a child's ways are not things to be threatened by, but rather cherished and preserved. Essentially, through this coming of age that occurs uniquely in the formative years, we are gifted to be the ones closest to them and thereby have a golden opportunity to allow this relationship to influence and change us into our finest selves.

To be sincerely emerging as an artful practitioner of humanity is to simply allow any and all of life's occupations to serve us through its teachings. For you, dear reader, all you need to do is reflect sincerely on what is happening now and be willing to allow it to be your finest schoolmaster, without reservation. I invite you to just be open to what you might see.

With that said, allow me to sum up the essence of this book in four simple phrases.

Forgive yourself.

Love your child.

Let change happen.

Right now.

About the Author

Brett Jordan, BSW, B.Msc., MSW, RSW, is an Ordained Minister and Registered Social Worker who has held a lifelong love affair with spirituality. His recent work has been focused in areas of personal mastery and resilience, with a special focus on inspiring emerging values and techniques for global co-leadership.

Brett is an avid researcher and philosopher in the field of spiritual maturity and his work is fueled by an intense curiosity about human behavior and the overarching role of the Divine in our lives.

Brett is also a homeschooling father. He lives with his wife Yiskah and their three sons in British Columbia, Canada.